ZURICH
TRAVEL GUIDE
2023

The most Updated pocket Guidebook:
A Panoramic Guide to Switzerland's Urban
Gem and Weaving Unforgettable Stories in
the Heart of Switzerland

MARCOS R. DORMAN

Zurich Travel Guide 2023

The most Updated pocket Guidebook:

A Panoramic Guide to Switzerland's Urban Gem and Weaving Unforgettable Stories in the Heart of Switzerland

By

Marcos R. Dorman

Table of content

My Vacation Trip To Zurich

Zurich, the biggest city in Switzerland, is recognized for its stunning surroundings, rich history, and active cultural scene. My recent holiday trip to Zurich was a genuinely remarkable experience that enabled me to immerse myself in the city's splendor, discover its historical landmarks, and appreciate its gastronomic pleasures. From the spectacular vistas of the Swiss Alps to the beautiful old town, Zurich offers a great combination of natural beauty and urban charm.

Exploring the Old Town:

One of the pleasures of my vacation was touring Zurich's lovely Old Town, known as Altstadt. As I went through cobblestone alleys, I was intrigued by the ancient buildings, small stores, and warm cafés that lined the tiny passageways. The Grossmünster and Fraumünster cathedrals, with their exquisite designs and centuries-old history, were awe-inspiring reminders of the city's cultural legacy. The clock face of St. Peter's Church was another masterpiece, affording a panoramic perspective of the city from its tower.

Lake Zurich and its Serenity:

The calm of Lake Zurich provides a quiet break from the hectic city life. The crystal-clear waters were surrounded by lush flora and scenic promenades, making it a wonderful site for a leisurely walk or a quiet boat ride. The view of the Alps reflected in the lake was a sight to see, particularly after sunset when the sky changed into a tapestry of vivid colors.

Culinary Delights:

Zurich's food scene was a fascinating trip of tastes and fragrances. I got the chance to sample classic Swiss delicacies such as fondue and raclette, experiencing the rich and decadent Swiss cheese culture firsthand. Exploring the local markets, I found a range of fresh vegetables, handcrafted chocolates, and pastries that were not only a pleasure for the taste senses but also a feast for the eyes.

Art and Culture:

Zurich's cultural attractions were similarly remarkable. I spent hours roaming around the Kunsthaus Zurich, an art museum that offers a wide collection of classics, spanning from Swiss painters to world greats like Picasso and Van Gogh. The museum provides insight into the growth of creative expression and its influence on society.

Day Trip to the Swiss Alps:

No vacation to Zurich would be complete without a day excursion to the gorgeous Swiss Alps. The modern Swiss transportation system made it simple to reach the alpine areas, where I found myself surrounded by towering peaks, shimmering snow, and fresh mountain air. The experience of riding a cable car to higher heights and soaking in panoramic sights was nothing short of stunning.

Swiss Punctuality and Precision:

One feature that jumped out during my journey was the Swiss adherence to timeliness and accuracy. From the flawless public transit system to the well-organized events and sights, Zurich's attention to efficiency was visible everywhere. This attention to detail brought an additional layer of comfort to my holiday, enabling me to make the most of my stay.

Conclusion:

My holiday trip to Zurich was a voyage of exploration, relaxation, and cultural enrichment. From the ancient charm of the Old Town to the tranquil serenity of Lake Zurich and the awe-inspiring Swiss Alps, every moment was filled with surprise and joy. The city's wonderful combination of heritage and technology, natural beauty, and urban elegance, left an unforgettable impact on my heart. As I went from Zurich, I brought with me memories that would continue to inspire and encourage me for years to come.

Chapter1:

Introduction to Zurich

Zurich, the biggest city in Switzerland, is a dynamic and culturally diverse destination that flawlessly integrates modernism with a deep-rooted past. Situated at the northern extremity of Lake Zurich and surrounded by the gorgeous Swiss Alps, this city provides a compelling experience for every sort of tourist. From its world-class museums and art galleries to its breathtaking natural surroundings and booming culinary scene, Zurich has something to offer everyone.

Historical and Cultural importance: Zurich has a history that extends back to Roman times, and its historical importance is apparent in its well-preserved medieval buildings and cobblestone streets. The city's Old Town, also known as Altstadt, is a maze of small lanes, lovely squares, and centuries-old buildings. The Grossmünster and Fraumünster churches, together with the St. Peter's Church, are not only architectural wonders but also transmitters of historical and cultural narratives. The city's museums, such as the Swiss National Museum and the Museum of Art (Kunsthaus Zürich), give insights into Switzerland's rich legacy and creative accomplishments.

Spectacular Scenery: Zurich's natural beauty is unrivaled. The tranquil Lake Zurich provides possibilities for boat rides, lakeside picnics, and strolls along its promenades. The adjacent Uetliberg Mountain affords a panoramic view of the whole city, the surrounding countryside, and the snow-capped Alps in the distance. The serene beauty of the city's parks, especially Lindenhof and the Botanical Garden, offers a relaxing getaway from the urban bustle.

Culinary Delights: Zurich's culinary scene is a gourmet trip that covers traditional Swiss tastes and a varied spectrum of other cuisines. From quaint cafés and street food markets to fancy Michelin-starred restaurants, the city caters to every appetite. Don't miss the opportunity to experience Swiss fondue, raclette, and chocolate — gastronomic delicacies that have become associated with Switzerland's character.

World-Class Shopping: For those inclined towards shopping, Zurich provides a choice of possibilities. The Bahnhofstrasse, one of the world's most prestigious shopping lanes, is dotted with luxury shops, worldwide brands, and department stores. Niederdorf, a lovely section inside the Old Town, is noted for its boutique shops, art galleries, and antique stores, great for discovering unique items.

Efficiency and Connectivity: Zurich's well-known Swiss efficiency is mirrored in its superb public transit infrastructure. The city's trams, buses, and trains operate with accuracy, making it simple to visit its different districts and attractions. Additionally, Zurich's prominence as a worldwide financial center offers great access for foreign passengers via its well-connected airport and railway station.

Year-Round Destination: Zurich is a city for all seasons. In the summer, you may enjoy open-air performances, lakeside activities, and outdoor eating. In winter, the city changes into a winter wonderland with Christmas markets and the opportunity for neighboring skiing and snowboarding trips.

Brief overview of Zurich's appeal and uniqueness

Nestled in the heart of Switzerland, Zurich stands as a tribute to the perfect mix of rich history and contemporary vitality. Its attractiveness and originality originate from a myriad of aspects that combined form a fascinating tapestry of culture, economy, and natural beauty. From its gorgeous scenery to its vibrant business sector, Zurich's attractiveness has no boundaries.

Historical Resilience: Zurich's origins stretch back to Roman times, and its historical architecture whispers stories of years gone by. The historic Old Town, with its cobblestone alleys and well-preserved buildings, leads tourists on a voyage through time. The Grossmünster and Fraumünster cathedrals stand as renowned buildings that have seen the city's evolution throughout the decades. This contrast of historical preservation in a contemporary metropolitan background is very remarkable.

Cultural Diversity: Zurich's attraction also resides in its global character. The city is a melting pot of cultures, bringing individuals from throughout the world. This variety is mirrored in the multiplicity of foreign cuisines, museums, galleries, and theatres. The Kunsthaus Zurich, home to treasures by Swiss and foreign artists, and the Rietberg Museum presenting non-European art illustrate the city's dedication to developing a worldwide cultural conversation.

Economic Powerhouse: Zurich's significance on the world economic scene is unmistakable. The city is a financial center, holding the headquarters of major multinational banks and financial organizations. Its stable economy and business-friendly climate have made it a magnet for international firms, entrepreneurs, and startups. The contrast of economic might against the background of the beautiful Lake Zurich says eloquently about the city's diverse attractiveness.

Natural Splendor: Zurich's particular attractiveness goes beyond its metropolitan setting. The city's gorgeous location on the beaches of Lake Zurich and the Limmat River is a sight to see. The adjacent Swiss Alps offer a spectacular background, making the city a gateway to outdoor experiences. Residents and tourists alike enjoy sports like hiking, skiing, and sailing, forging a profound link between urban life and the natural environment.

Quality of Life: One of Zurich's most alluring qualities is its outstanding quality of life. The city routinely scores high in worldwide quality of living indices because of its outstanding healthcare, education, and public transit systems. The focus on sustainability and green areas helps the general well-being of its citizens. This devotion to a high level of life generates an atmosphere that is both beautiful and caring.

Innovation and Education: Zurich's universities and research institutes have nurtured an atmosphere of innovation. The Swiss Federal Institute of Technology (ETH Zurich) serves as a beacon of scientific and technical innovation. The city's innovation hubs and startup incubators encourage creativity and attract forward-thinking people from many disciplines. This culture of innovation maintains Zurich's continuous importance on the world stage.

Year-round Allure: Zurich's attraction is not tied to any one season. Each period of the year gives a distinct experience. Whether it's the vivid summer festivals by the lake, the beautiful foliage of autumn in the parks, the festive Christmas markets in winter, or the flowering of spring flowers, Zurich captivates tourists with its ever-changing but persistent attractiveness.

Useful travel tips for visitors

Zurich, a lovely city set in the heart of Switzerland, is recognized for its breathtaking scenery, rich history, and dynamic cultural scene. Whether you're traveling for business or pleasure, this guide gives important recommendations to ensure your trip to Zurich is both pleasurable and memorable.

1. Transportation:

Zurich features an efficient and dependable public transportation system. The trams, buses, and trains are well-connected, making it simple to explore the city and its surroundings.

Consider getting a Zurich Card, which gives unlimited travel on public transit throughout the city and savings on museum entries. It's a cost-effective method to explore and enjoy the city.

2. Currency:

Switzerland uses the Swiss Franc (CHF) as its currency. While credit cards are frequently accepted, it's important to have some cash on hand, particularly for minor transactions or businesses that may not take cards.

3. Language:

The official languages of Zurich are German, French, and Italian. English is also frequently spoken, particularly in tourist areas, hotels, and restaurants.

4. Weather:

Zurich features a moderate climate, with distinct seasons. Pack properly, considering the weather during your vacation. Layers are crucial, since the weather may change suddenly.

5. Tipping:

Tipping at restaurants and cafés is not necessary, since service costs are frequently included. However, rounding up the amount or giving a little tip is appreciated. For great service, a 10% tip is considered generous.

6. Cultural Etiquette:

Swiss culture appreciates timeliness, so be on time for appointments, bookings, and excursions.

Politeness is highly praised. Greet locals with a "Grüezi" (hello) and utilize "Bitte" (please) and "Danke" (thank you) throughout your conversations.

7. Water Quality:

Tap water in Zurich is of great quality and is safe to drink. Carry a reusable water bottle to remain hydrated while exploring.

8. Shopping:

Bahnhofstrasse is one of the world's most prestigious shopping lanes, including high-end shops and department stores. Remember that stores shut early on Saturdays and are normally closed on Sundays.

9. Cultural Sites:

Zurich features various museums and galleries. The Kunsthaus Zurich has an amazing collection of artworks, while the Swiss National Museum gives insights into Switzerland's history.

The Old Town (Altstadt) is a treasure trove of medieval buildings, beautiful streets, and historical attractions.

10. Day Trips:

Use Zurich as a base to visit neighboring sights. Take a beautiful train trip to Lucerne, explore the gorgeous town of Zermatt with its famed Matterhorn mountain, or take a boat tour on Lake Zurich.

11. Cuisine:

Swiss cuisine is varied and influenced by surrounding nations. Don't miss out on eating classic foods like fondue and raclette. Vegetarians and vegans will also find many eating alternatives.

12. Safety:

Zurich is considered a secure place for vacationers. However, be careful with your valuables, particularly in busy locations, to prevent petty theft.

13. Time Zone:

Zurich follows Central European Time (CET), UTC+1, and Central European Summer Time (CEST), UTC+2 during daylight saving time.

14. Wi-Fi and Connectivity:

Many cafés, hotels, and public locations provide free Wi-Fi. You might also try obtaining a local SIM card for your phone to keep connected.

15. Events and Festivals:

Check the local event calendar before your trip. Zurich holds several cultural events, music festivals, and exhibits throughout the year.

Chapter 2:

Getting Ready for Zurich

Zurich, the dynamic and scenic city tucked in the heart of Switzerland, is a location where medieval architecture meets contemporary refinement. With its beautiful lakes, lush landscapes, and rich cultural legacy, Zurich provides a unique combination of tradition and innovation that captivates tourists from across the globe. Whether you're planning a relaxed vacation or a business trip, getting ready for Zurich is a thrilling experience in itself.

Exploring the Essentials:
Before going on your Zurich vacation, it's necessary to obtain knowledge about the city's major elements. Zurich's efficient public transit system comprises trains, trams, and buses, making it simple to travel to the city and its surroundings. The Swiss

Franc (CHF) is the local currency, so it's a good idea to have some cash on hand for little transactions, but credit cards are generally accepted.

Cultural Sensitivity:

Switzerland, notably Zurich, prides itself on its cultural variety and friendliness. The folks are often reserved yet kind. When dealing with locals, a friendly grin and a simple "Grüezi" (hello in Swiss German) go a long way. It's also crucial to educate oneself about local traditions and etiquette to guarantee a courteous and enjoyable visit.

Weather Preparedness:
Zurich enjoys four unique seasons, each bringing its beauty. Summers (June to August) are pleasant, with temperatures ranging from 20°C to 25°C (68°F to 77°F). Autumn (September to November) delivers beautiful foliage and pleasant weather, while winter (December to February) buries the

city in snow and gives the chance for winter sports aficionados to tackle the surrounding slopes. Spring (March to May) sees the city come alive with blooms. Packing proper attire for the season is crucial for comfort and pleasure.

Savoring Swiss Cuisine:
Swiss cuisine is a beautiful combination of influences from numerous locations, resulting in a rich and exquisite gastronomic environment. Zurich's cuisine scene includes fondue, raclette, rösti, and exquisite Swiss chocolate. Don't miss the opportunity to sample these classic meals at local eateries, ranging from modest cafés to upmarket restaurants.

Exploring Attractions:
Zurich provides a choice of attractions that appeal to varied interests. For art connoisseurs, the Kunsthaus Zurich showcases an excellent collection of European art. The Old Town (Altstadt) with

its cobblestone lanes, ancient houses, and lovely squares is a must-visit for history aficionados. The historic Bahnhofstrasse offers world-class shopping, while Lake Zurich provides a quiet location for leisure.

Language Considerations:
While Swiss German is the most generally spoken language in Zurich, English is also regularly used, particularly in tourist areas. Learning a few simple words in Swiss German may enrich your trip and display your appreciation for the local culture.

Embracing Sustainability:

Zurich's dedication to sustainability is obvious in its efficient public transit, recycling programs, and green areas. Embrace local habits by taking public transit and limiting your ecological imprint throughout your trip.

Planning:

To make the most of your vacation, try crafting an itinerary that incorporates both major destinations and hidden treasures. Research events, festivals, and exhibits taking place during your stay to immerse yourself in the city's cultural environment.

Pre-trip planning: visas, currency, weather

Traveling to Zurich, the busy and scenic city in Switzerland takes meticulous pre-trip preparation to guarantee a smooth and comfortable experience. This note will walk you through crucial areas of your pre-trip preparations, including visas, currency conversion, and weather concerns.

Visa Requirements: Switzerland is part of the Schengen Area, which provides visa-free travel for nationals of numerous countries, including the United States, Canada, the European Union member states, Australia, and more. Citizens of these countries may normally remain in Switzerland for up to 90 days during 180 days for tourist or business reasons without having a visa. However, it's vital to examine the precise visa requirements for your nation before traveling. If you want to remain longer or for other reasons like a job or study, you may need to apply for a different sort of visa.

Currency Exchange: The official currency of Switzerland is the Swiss Franc (CHF). While major credit cards are frequently accepted in Zurich, it's a good idea to have some Swiss Francs on hand for little transactions and establishments that may not take cards. Before your travel, check the conversion rate and consider converting a modest amount of money at your local bank or currency exchange agency for ease upon arrival. You may also withdraw cash from ATMs in Zurich, but be mindful of any related costs. Remember that Switzerland is notorious for its high living expenses, so prepare your budget appropriately.

Weather & Packing: Zurich has a moderate environment with different seasons, making it vital to carry suitable attire for the weather throughout your stay. Summers (June to August) are often warm, with average temperatures ranging from 17°C to 25°C (63°F to 77°F). Light and breathable clothes, sunglasses, sunscreen, and a hat are advised. Don't forget a light jacket or sweater for chilly nights.

In contrast, winters (December to February) may be rather cold, with temperatures averaging approximately -1°C to 5°C (30°F to 41°F). If you're coming at this time, take thick layers, a heavy coat, gloves, a scarf, and strong waterproof boots. Spring (March to May) and fall (September to November) provide gentler temperatures, although packing layers is still suggested, since the weather may be unpredictable.

Rainfall is likely throughout the year, so taking a small umbrella or a waterproof jacket with a hood is a smart idea. A solid pair of walking shoes is also important to tour Zurich comfortably, particularly if you wish to enjoy its abundant outdoor attractions.

Packing tips for different seasons

Zurich, the bustling and scenic city set in the heart of Switzerland, provides a wealth of activities throughout the year. With its attractive architecture, spectacular lakeside vistas, and a combination of old-world charm and modernity, Zurich is a place that lures tourists in every season. However, owing to its varied environment, preparing adequately for each season is vital to make the most of your vacation. Here are some packing recommendations to help you manage the varied seasons in Zurich.

Spring (March to May): Spring in Zurich is a period of regeneration and waking. As the city emerges from the winter months, the weather may be rather erratic. Here's what to pack:

Layers: Spring temperatures might change, so bring a range of clothing layers such as light sweaters, cardigans, and long-sleeve shirts. These may be simply added or withdrawn depending on the temperature.

Rain Gear: Spring rains are typical, so a small umbrella and a waterproof jacket are needed. Don't forget waterproof shoes or boots for exploring without getting your feet wet.

Comfortable Strolling Shoes: Zurich is best visited on foot, so pack comfortable shoes ideal for strolling on cobblestone streets and rough terrain.

Light Scarf & Accessories: A light scarf not only gives a touch of flair but may also offer an additional layer of warmth when required. Don't forget sunglasses and a flexible hat.

Summer (June to August): Zurich comes alive throughout the summer months with outdoor activities, festivals, and vibrant café culture. The weather is normally warm and pleasant, however, there are a few things to consider:

Light apparel: Pack a combination of lightweight, breathable apparel such as shorts, dresses, t-shirts, and skirts. Also, pack a few somewhat dressier alternatives for nights out.

Swimwear: Zurich features numerous gorgeous lakes, and having a refreshing plunge is a common summer pastime. Bring swimsuits and a beach blanket for a pleasant lakeside experience.

Sun Protection: The sun may be intense, so carry sunscreen, a wide-brimmed hat, and sunglasses to defend yourself from the sun's rays.

Compact Day Bag: A compact backpack or crossbody bag is perfect for transporting necessities while you tour the city, attend festivals, or take day excursions.

Autumn (September to November): Autumn in Zurich presents a stunning display of colors as the leaves change. The weather starts to drop down, and the city becomes quieter after the summer rush:

Warm Layers: As the temps drop, carry sweaters, cardigans, and light jackets. It's a good idea to have adaptable items that you can simply mix and match.

Rain Gear: Like spring, fall may bring rainy days, so ensure you have an umbrella, a waterproof jacket, and proper footwear.

Fall Accessories: Embrace the season with comfy accessories such as scarves, gloves, and a beanie to remain warm.

Winter (December to February): Winter in Zurich turns the city into a snowy paradise, giving chances for winter sports and festive celebrations:

Winter clothes: Pack warm clothes such as thick coats, insulated jackets, sweaters, and thermal underwear. Layering is crucial to remaining comfortable.

Winter Accessories: Don't forget gloves, a scarf, and a hat to keep oneself warm whether browsing outdoor Christmas markets or enjoying winter sports.

Footwear: Sturdy, waterproof boots with decent grip are required for negotiating icy streets and maybe indulging in winter sports.

Electrical Adapters: Switzerland utilizes a different sort of electrical socket, so ensure to take the right adapters for your electronics.

By adapting your packing list to the individual season, you can assure a comfortable and pleasurable vacation to Zurich, no matter the weather. Remember to check the weather prediction before your trip and make modifications to your packing list appropriately. With the correct wardrobe and necessities, you'll be well-prepared to experience the particular charm of Zurich in any season.

Health and safety considerations

policies, programs, and cultural aspects that contribute to its reputation as a safe and healthy place to live.

Urban Planning and Infrastructure:
One of the underlying elements of Zurich's great health and safety record is its rigorous urban planning and infrastructure development. The city is noted for its efficient transportation infrastructure, including an extensive network of trains, trams, and buses that decreases traffic congestion and promotes the use of public transit. This not only improves air quality but also decreases the likelihood of accidents.

Zurich's dedication to pedestrian-friendly streets and bike lanes encourages a better lifestyle and safer means of transportation. Properly maintained roads and pathways, well-lit public places, and well-marked crossings promote the safety of walkers and cyclists, limiting the likelihood of accidents.

Emergency Services and Preparedness:
Zurich's strong emergency services play a critical role in protecting the safety of its citizens. The city has a well-coordinated network of emergency response units, including police, fire, and medical services. This fast response system is supported by innovative technology and well-trained individuals, guaranteeing swift and effective help during crises.

In addition to quick emergency services, Zurich puts a great focus on catastrophe preparation. Regular exercises and simulations are held to assess the city's preparation for different situations, ranging from natural catastrophes to industrial mishaps. This preemptive strategy strengthens the city's capacity to manage emergencies and safeguard its citizens.

Healthcare Facilities and Access:

Access to excellent healthcare is a crucial component of a safe and healthy community. Zurich features a modern healthcare system that provides extensive medical services to its citizens. The city is home to world-class hospitals, clinics, and medical research institutes, providing a broad variety of specialized treatments and cutting-edge technology. This accessibility to healthcare adds to the general well-being of Zurich's citizens, ensuring that they get prompt and adequate medical treatment.

Environmental Sustainability:

Zurich's dedication to environmental sustainability coincides with its emphasis on health and safety. The city stresses clean air and water quality via tough laws and ecologically responsible policies. Efforts to decrease pollution, create green areas, and encourage sustainable habits contribute to the general health of both the people and the environment.

Cultural Factors:

Zurich's high health and safety standards are also affected by cultural characteristics strongly ingrained in Swiss culture. The Swiss respect accuracy, discipline, and devotion to norms, which extends to concerns of public safety. This cultural perspective fosters responsible conduct and obedience to legislation, leading to a safer urban environment.

Community Engagement:

Community involvement and participation play a critical role in sustaining health and safety standards. Zurich supports public engagement via venues such as neighborhood groups and town hall meetings. This open forum enables citizens to express concerns, offer input on safety problems, and cooperate with authorities to discover effective solutions.

Chapter 3:

Navigating Zurich

Nestled within the stunning landscapes of Switzerland, Zurich stands as a classic combination of old-world charm and cutting-edge innovation. This flourishing city, with its rich history, cultural vitality, and economic strength, provides a captivating experience to both inhabitants and tourists. Navigating Zurich is a trip that takes you through its historic districts, world-class institutions, magnificent natural surroundings, and efficient transit system.

Historic Quarters:
Zurich's historic districts relate stories of the past while living seamlessly with current urban life. The historic Old Town, or "Altstadt," is a tangle of small lanes, cobblestone streets, and well-preserved

houses. Here, the Grossmünster and Fraumünster churches remain as quiet witnesses to centuries of history. Climbing the towers of these cathedrals rewards you with magnificent views over the city's roofs and the tranquil waters of Lake Zurich.

Cultural Enclaves:

Zurich's cultural environment is active and diversified, appealing to every taste and interest. The Kunsthaus Zurich, one of Switzerland's most recognized art museums, features an extraordinary collection of artworks by Swiss and foreign artists spanning numerous centuries. For individuals captivated by science and technology, the Swiss Museum of Transport provides an interactive overview of the country's transportation history.

Lake Zurich:

Lake Zurich's crystal-clear waters create a beautiful backdrop for leisure and relaxation. The lake's banks are ornamented with parks, promenades, and recreational amenities. Taking a boat tour on the lake is a lovely way to admire the city's skyline and the surrounding Alpine beauty. During summers, residents and visitors alike throng to the lake's beaches for swimming, sunbathing, and water sports.

Efficient Transportation:
Zurich features an extraordinarily efficient public transit infrastructure that makes around the city a snap. The trams, buses, and trains run with Swiss precision, linking every part of the city and spreading to its suburbs. The Swiss Travel Pass allows travelers unrestricted access to the public transportation network, making it an inexpensive and handy alternative for visiting Zurich and beyond.

Culinary Delights:
Zurich's gastronomy culture is a reflection of its worldwide influence and local traditions. From intimate fondue restaurants that warm

the heart with melting cheese to slick gourmet diners stretching culinary frontiers, the city caters to every palette. Don't forget to sample the wonderful Swiss chocolate, which is a genuine reflection of Swiss workmanship and attention to excellence.

Innovation Hub:
Beyond its historical and cultural characteristics, Zurich stands as a worldwide center for innovation and finance. The city has a multitude of global firms, startups, and research organizations. The ETH Zurich, one of the world's finest technological institutions, has produced several Nobel laureates and pioneers in different disciplines.

Festivals & Events:

Zurich's event calendar is overflowing with events that celebrate art, culture, music, and more. The Zurich Film Festival draws filmmakers and aficionados from across the globe, while Street Parade turns the city into a bustling dance floor with electronic music and colorful floats. During the joyful Christmas season, the city's marketplaces and streets glitter with lights and seasonal happiness.

Overview of Zurich's public transportation system

Zurich, the biggest city in Switzerland, is recognized for its efficient, dependable, and extensive public transit system. The city's dedication to sustainable transportation, along with its well-integrated network of trains, trams, buses, and boats, makes it an example for other metropolitan centers across the globe. This article presents a detailed analysis of Zurich's public transportation system, stressing its essential features, advantages, and reasons for its success.

1. ** **Integration and interconnection: Zurich's public transportation system is marked by its extraordinary integration and interconnection. The Swiss Travel System, a concerted effort between multiple transport providers, facilitates seamless transitions between various kinds of transportation. This comprises trains, trams, buses, and even boats, all operating on a single, unified fare system. Passengers may smoothly move between various modes, giving flexibility and convenience in their everyday journeys.

2. ** **Reliability and timeliness: The Swiss are recognized for their timeliness, and Zurich's public transit system is a perfect illustration of this cultural quality. Trains, trams, and buses run with extraordinary accuracy, following strict timetables. This stability is vital for the city's running, allowing inhabitants and tourists to plan their travels with certainty.

**3. ** Comprehensive Coverage: Zurich's public transit network covers practically every area of the city and extends to the outlying regions. This wide coverage decreases the dependency on private automobiles, minimizes congestion, and contributes to a better environment. Residents may visit their businesses, educational institutions, recreational locations, and cultural venues with ease, generating a feeling of accessibility for everyone.

**4. ** Sustainability and Environmental Impact: The city's focus on sustainability and environmental awareness is evident in its transportation system. Zurich's public transportation fleet contains energy-efficient vehicles, and the integration of electric buses and trams has been emphasized. This commitment to reduce emissions coincides with Switzerland's broader efforts to fight climate change and promote healthier air quality.

5. ** **Innovation and modernization: Zurich's transportation system consistently embraces innovation and modernization. The development of digital technologies, such as smartphone applications for route planning, real-time information, and electronic ticketing, has boosted passenger experience. These innovations provide travelers with the knowledge required to traverse the city effectively.

6. ** **Swiss Quality and Safety: The Swiss reputation for quality and safety extends to its transportation system. Cleanliness, upkeep, and security are vital. Well-lit stations, clean cars, and clear signs add to an overall nice commuting experience.

7. ** **Tourism and Economy: Zurich's efficient public transportation system plays a crucial role in supporting the city's tourism and economy. Visitors may readily explore the city's attractions utilizing the transit network, generating tourism earnings. Additionally, the system's dependability encourages people to travel for employment and recreation, encouraging economic activity across the area.

**8. ** Community Benefits: Zurich's public transit system stimulates social contact and a feeling of community. Passengers from diverse walks of life use the same forms of transportation, encouraging inclusion and a sense of camaraderie. This community feature coincides with Switzerland's focus on cohesiveness and social harmony.

**9. ** Obstacles and Future Developments: Despite its triumphs, Zurich's transportation system confronts obstacles. With a rising population and greater demand, preserving efficiency and capacity remains a concern. The city seeks to further boost sustainability by increasing electric mobility alternatives and incorporating additional renewable energy sources.

10. ** **Lessons for Other Cities: Zurich's public transportation system offers a significant model for other cities aiming to establish sustainable, efficient, and user-friendly transit networks. Key insights include the significance of integration, accurate scheduling, environmental concern, and continual investment in modernization.

Tips for using trams, buses, and trains

Zurich, the gorgeous Swiss city cradled by the clean waters of Lake Zurich and encircled by the magnificent Alps, is famed for its efficient and large public transit network. Trams, buses, and trains effortlessly link the city, allowing inhabitants and tourists alike a convenient way to enjoy its rich cultural legacy, breathtaking landscapes, and dynamic urban life. To make the most of your travel, here are some helpful recommendations for utilizing trams, buses, and trains in Zurich.

1. Purchase the Right Ticket: Before going on your trip, confirm you have the necessary ticket. Zurich's public transit relies on a zone-based fare structure. Tickets may be bought from vending machines, online, or through mobile applications. Choose from single-ride, day-pass, or multiple-ride choices depending on your travel plans and length of stay.

2. Validate Your Ticket: For trams and buses, you'll normally find ticket validation machines inside the vehicle or at stations. Make sure you confirm your ticket before boarding to avoid a penalty. Train tickets frequently don't need validation since they're time-stamped when bought.

3. Respect the Timetable: Zurich is recognized for its timeliness, and its public transport system is no exception. Trams, buses, and trains adhere to rigid timetables. Arrive a few minutes before departure to guarantee you don't miss your transport.

4. Efficient Transfers: Transfers between trams, buses, and trains are supposed to be smooth. Make sure you're informed of the connections and transfer places for your route. Large stations like Zurich Hauptbahnhof (the main railway station) have good signs and maps to help you.

5. Explore ZVV Zones: Zurich's transport network is separated into distinct zones. Your ticket's validity depends on the zones you go through. The city itself normally falls inside Zone 110. If you wish to journey farther, such as to Uetliberg Mountain, check if your ticket includes the relevant zones.

6. Travel cards and Cards: For prolonged visits or frequent travel, consider acquiring travel cards like the Zurich Card or the ZürichCARD. These give unlimited trips on public transit within particular zones, coupled with discounts on museums and attractions.

7. Accessibility Matters: Zurich's public transport system is well-equipped for accessibility. Trams, buses, and many railway stations have amenities like ramps and specific places for those with impaired mobility. Look out for the wheelchair icon on vehicles and platforms.

8. Night Network: Zurich's night network guarantees you can explore the city even after dark. Night buses and trams operate at decreased frequency but cover essential routes, enabling you to enjoy Zurich's nightlife and nighttime activities easily.

9. Use Maps and applications: Utilize Zurich's official transit applications and internet tools. These give real-time information on timetables, delays, and routes, and even provide a map tool to assist you navigate about the city with ease.

10. Be Mindful of Quiet Zones: Some railway compartments and trams have designated quiet zones, where passengers are required to keep a reduced level. If you want a calmer flying experience, these zones are excellent for rest or business.

11. Biking and Public Transport: Zurich is a bicycle-friendly city. Many trams and buses have bike racks, and you may transport your bike on trains outside of peak hours. This connection makes it possible to mix bicycles with public transit for a flexible travel experience.

12. Children and Families: Public transit in Zurich is family-friendly. Kids under a specific age typically travel for free or at discounted costs. Many trams and buses also have allocated sections for strollers.

13. Safety and Etiquette: Respect the laws of public transit etiquette, such as giving up seats to the elderly or pregnant, keeping noise levels down, and abstaining from eating or drinking in vehicles.

Information on Zurich Card and other travel passes

Zurich, frequently touted as the financial and cultural heart of Switzerland, features an intriguing combination of modernism and history. The city is recognized for its excellent public transit system and a myriad of travel passes that make accessing Zurich's attractions a pleasure. Among them, the Zurich Card stands out as a wonderful companion for travelers seeking both ease and savings. In addition to the Zurich Card, various additional travel permits provide unique opportunities for seeing not only Zurich but also the whole nation.

Zurich Card:
Unveiling Convenience and Savings

The Zurich Card is a comprehensive travel permit that opens the door to an assortment of incentives for tourists. Whether you're a cultural aficionado, an active adventurer, or just seeking to make the most of your stay in Zurich, the Zurich Card is intended to adapt to your requirements.

Key Features:

Unlimited Public Transportation: The Zurich Card allows unlimited access to the city's public transportation system, including trams, buses, trains, and boats. This unlimited mobility enables you to smoothly navigate between attractions and communities.

Free Museum access: Culture fans will find the Zurich Card especially intriguing since it grants free access to over 40 institutions in the city. From the famous Kunsthaus Zurich to the FIFA World Football Museum, the card offers a broad variety of cultural events.

Discounts: Alongside gratis entrance to museums, the card gives discounts on numerous attractions, trips, and even selected shops and restaurants. This makes it a useful tool for budget-conscious vacationers.

Airport Transfer: The Zurich Card extends its convenience to your arrival, delivering a free 2nd class rail ticket from Zurich Airport to the city center, enabling you to commence your tour straight away.

Validity Options: The Zurich Card is available for 24, 72, or 96 hours, allowing you freedom in selecting the term that coincides with your travel plans.

Other Travel Passes: Discovering Switzerland
While the Zurich Card is great for a Zurich-focused journey, Switzerland's efficient transportation network begs guests to explore beyond its bounds. Several travel tickets provide appealing possibilities to dig deeper into the country's magnificent landscapes.

1. Swiss Travel Permit: The Swiss Travel Pass is a comprehensive permit that provides unrestricted travel on trains, buses, and boats in Switzerland. It also provides free access to over 500 museums and gives savings on mountain trips.

2. Half Fare Card: As the name implies, this card enables you to buy tickets for trains, trams, buses, and boats for half price. It's a good alternative if you're planning many long-distance travels.

3. Tell-Pass: Perfect for individuals who wish to experience the heart of Switzerland, the Tell-Pass covers travel in Central Switzerland and includes boats, trains, buses, and certain mountain cable cars.

4. Regional Passes: Switzerland's varied regions provide their distinctive passes. The Berner Oberland Regional Pass, for example, focuses on the Bernese Oberland region, covering the magnificent Jungfrau area.

5. Swiss Family Card: Families traveling with children may benefit from the Swiss Family Card, which enables children under 16 to travel for free when accompanied by at least one adult holding a Swiss Travel Pass.

Making an Informed Choice

As you plan your vacation to Zurich and Switzerland, carefully consider your travel interests and the sights you intend to experience. The Zurich Card is a terrific alternative for a focused Zurich experience, delivering convenience, cultural immersion, and savings. If your wanderlust goes beyond Zurich's city boundaries, browse the different travel pass choices that fit your plan, whether it's exploring the scenic countryside or climbing the spectacular Swiss Alps. With these travel cards in hand, your Swiss journey is primed to be a flawless and enjoyable experience.

Chapter 4:

Exploring Zurich's Neighborhoods

Nestled in the heart of Switzerland, Zurich is a city that flawlessly integrates modernism with history, providing a diversity of districts that appeal to varied interests and lifestyles. From the busy metropolitan atmosphere of the city center to the calm and gorgeous places along the beaches of Lake Zurich, the city's neighborhoods provide something for everyone. This excursion takes us through some of Zurich's intriguing districts, each with its particular charm and character.

1. Old Town (Altstadt):
Zurich's Old Town, with its cobblestone alleys and medieval buildings, is a voyage back in time. The tiny lanes, picturesque squares, and antique buildings create a

wonderful environment. The Grossmünster and Fraumünster cathedrals stand as recognizable icons, while Niederdorf provides a dynamic mix of cafés, shops, and galleries. The Old Town is a living testimony to Zurich's rich legacy.

2. Kreis 5 (Zürich West):

Once an industrial zone, Zürich West has turned into a powerhouse of creativity and innovation. Trendy art galleries, repurposed factories, and design studios have taken root here. The Prime Tower and Viadukt are contemporary architectural wonders, and the colorful Im Viadukt market provides a gourmet excursion. The area's regeneration is a monument to Zurich's vibrant character.

3. Seefeld:

Nestled along the shores of Lake Zurich, Seefeld is associated with calm and luxury. The promenade provides spectacular lake vistas, while the Opera House lends a touch of refinement. Quaint shops, high-end restaurants, and attractive gardens create an atmosphere of elegant relaxation. Seefeld embodies the city's beautiful combination of nature and culture.

4. Wiedikon:

For a taste of local life, Wiedikon is a wonderful trip. This residential area has a warm, neighborhood atmosphere. Diverse markets, friendly cafés, and small businesses give a true Zurich experience. The lovely Bullingerplatz area acts as a meeting spot for inhabitants. Wiedikon shows the warmth and familiarity that Zurich provides to its citizens.

5. Enge:

Enge is a beautiful combination of domestic charm and urban convenience. With its closeness to the lake, parks, and cultural institutions, it appeals to both nature lovers and culture fanatics. The Museum Rietberg and the spacious Sihlpark give interesting experiences. Enge serves as an emblem of Zurich's dedication to great living.

6. Albisrieden:

Albisrieden offers a mix between suburban serenity and metropolitan connectedness. Its tree-lined lanes, charming cafés, and small markets provide a flavor of suburban life. The Uetliberg mountain offers chances for outdoor sports and magnificent views. Albisrieden highlights Zurich's capacity to create varied living situations within its bounds.

7. Höngg:

Nestled on the western slopes of Zurich, Höngg provides a calm getaway from the daily bustle. Its lovely village vibe is complimented by historical buildings like the Hönggerberg Castle. Lützelhof Park and the neighboring Limmat River provide green places for recreation. Höngg illustrates Zurich's dedication to preserving its historical origins while embracing modernity.

Description of popular neighborhoods: Old Town (Altstadt), Niederdorf, Bahnhofstrasse, etc.

Zurich, the biggest city in Switzerland, is recognized for its scenic scenery, cultural legacy, and active districts. Among these areas, Old Town (Altstadt), Niederdorf, and Bahnhofstrasse stand out as intriguing places that present a unique combination of history, modernity, and various experiences. This article digs into the particular traits and charm of these prominent Zurich districts.

Old Town (Altstadt): Preserving the Past

Old Town, also known as Altstadt, serves as the heart and spirit of Zurich. This area is a monument to the city's rich history and cultural heritage. As one wanders through the cobblestone streets and twisting lanes, the architecture from different ages provides a tale of Zurich's development. The medieval beauty is obvious, with magnificently maintained structures, some going back to the 12th century. The Grossmünster und Fraumünster cathedrals, renowned icons, rise magnificently, showing architectural magnificence.

Altstadt isn't simply a historic enclave; it's a thriving center of activity. The tiny lanes are dotted with an eclectic mix of shops, art galleries, cafés, and classic Swiss cuisine. The Niederdorf district of Old Town is especially recognized for its dynamic nightlife, where residents and visitors congregate to enjoy live music, gastronomic delights, and a lively environment.

Niederdorf: Where Past Meets Present

Niederdorf, hidden inside Old Town, displays a unique character of its own. This bohemian area harmoniously integrates history with contemporary, creating a compelling ambiance. During the day, the streets are abuzz with shoppers discovering unique stores, craftsmen showing their crafts, and cafés serving wonderful delights. The Rathaus Café, housed in a historic structure, offers a tranquil place to enjoy a cup of coffee while taking in the surroundings.

As the sun sets, Niederdorf evolves into a hub for entertainment. The neighborhood comes alive with clubs, taverns, and restaurants, each oozing its distinct character. Whether you're a lover of jazz music or modern art, or just desire to enjoy the joyous vibe, Niederdorf offers something for everyone.

Bahnhofstrasse: A Shopper's Paradise

In sharp contrast to the historical ambiance of Old Town and Niederdorf, Bahnhofstrasse showcases Zurich's contemporary and cosmopolitan side. This luxury retail area is famous internationally for its lavish products. With flagship shops of worldwide fashion labels, haute couture boutiques, and superb jewelry outlets, Bahnhofstrasse is a wonderland for fashion fans and connoisseurs of refinement.

The avenue spans from Zurich's major train station to Lake Zurich, providing a seamless combination of retail and recreation. High-end department shops like Jelmoli and Globus offer a varied selection of merchandise, from fashion to gourmet delights. The ambiance of Bahnhofstrasse is unmistakably cosmopolitan, drawing people from throughout the globe who seek the ultimate luxury and elegance.

The Essence of Zurich's Neighborhoods

In conclusion, the districts of Old Town (Altstadt), Niederdorf, and Bahnhofstrasse jointly express the core of Zurich's identity. Old Town exhibits the city's historical origins and architectural magnificence. Niederdorf connects the past and contemporary, providing a diverse combination of shopping, eating, and entertainment. Bahnhofstrasse, on the other hand, embodies contemporary luxury and upmarket retail, catering to individuals with a flair for refinement.

Each of these areas has a distinct narrative to tell, adding to Zurich's colorful and compelling urban fabric. As tourists stroll the old streets of Altstadt, immerse themselves in Niederdorf's creative spirit, and enjoy the splendor of Bahnhofstrasse, they discover the numerous characteristics that make Zurich a genuinely beautiful place.

Highlighting each area's unique attractions, dining, and shopping

Nestled in the heart of Switzerland, Zurich, a city famed for its mix of old-world beauty and modern energy, draws tourists with its numerous attractions. From enthralling sites that span centuries of history to culinary experiences that tickle the taste senses, and a retail scene that is both elegant and diverse, Zurich is a treasure trove waiting to be found.

Attractions:
A Window into Zurich's Rich Heritage

The streets of Zurich are lined with history, and its attractions serve as windows into its legendary past. The Old Town (Altstadt), a tangle of cobblestone streets and ancient buildings, is a refuge for history buffs. Stroll around the lovely streets, taking in the Rathaus (Town Hall) with its ornate façade, and visit the Grossmünster and Fraumünster churches, each with its architectural style and great historical importance.

For individuals seeking creative enlightenment, the Kunsthaus Zurich is a refuge of exquisite art. Home to an exceptional collection of Swiss and worldwide treasures, including works by Alberto Giacometti and Marc Chagall, the museum is a cultural jewel that symbolizes Zurich's love for creation.

Lake Zurich and the neighboring parks provide a tranquil getaway from metropolitan life. The lake's beautiful waters offer the ideal background for a leisurely boat excursion, while the parks enable tourists to relax and enjoy picnics or strolls.

Dining:
A Gastronomic Journey Through Zurich's Flavors

Zurich's culinary scene is a combination of history and innovation, appealing to every palette. Begin your gastronomic tour with a visit to the Lindenhofkeller, a historic restaurant located in a 14th-century structure. Indulge in classic Swiss delicacies like fondue and raclette, savoring the country's distinct tastes.

For a modern spin, head into Zurich's hip areas like Kreis 4 and 5. Here, you'll discover a diversity of ethnic eateries, from Asian fusion to Middle Eastern treats. Sample foreign cuisine while taking in the young spirit of these bustling locales.

No visit to Zurich is complete without a trip to the Confiserie Sprüngli. This classic Swiss bakery impresses guests with its scrumptious Luxemburgerli macaroons and velvety hot chocolate — a wonderful feast for the senses.

Shopping:
From Boutiques to Luxury Flagships

Zurich provides a shopping experience that appeals to all interests, from high-end luxury shopping to eccentric shops. The Bahnhofstrasse, one of the world's most prestigious shopping districts, features a selection of major luxury brands and department shops. Lose yourself in a world of luxury as you tour iconic boutiques from Louis Vuitton to Rolex.

For a more handmade ambiance, try the Niederdorf District. This neighborhood is a hotspot for interesting boutiques, galleries, and antique stores. Discover one-of-a-kind treasures, from handcrafted jewelry to antique discoveries, as you walk through its beautiful alleyways.

Zurich West features an edgier retail environment, with renovated industrial premises holding trendy boutiques, modern design stores, and local concept shops. Embrace Zurich's contemporary look as you explore this lively district.

Chapter 5:

Top Attractions in Zurich

Nestled in the heart of Switzerland, Zurich is a city that flawlessly mixes its rich past with its modern metropolitan attractiveness. From the calm beaches of Lake Zurich to the lively cultural scene, the city provides a compelling combination of activities that appeal to all interests. This article begins on a trip to identify the top attractions that make Zurich a must-visit location.

Old Town (Altstadt): Zurich's Old Town is a time capsule that takes tourists ages ago. Cobblestone streets run past medieval buildings, leading to lovely squares and historical attractions. The Grossmünster and Fraumünster cathedrals tower tall, their elaborate construction representing the city's religious tradition. The small lanes, filled with colorful stores, art galleries, and quiet cafés, give a fascinating tour through the city's past.

Bahnhofstrasse: For shopaholics and those with an eye for luxury, Bahnhofstrasse is a wonderland. recognized as one of the world's most exclusive shopping districts, this boulevard is dotted with high-end shops, department stores, and recognized brands. Even if shopping isn't on the plan, a stroll along Bahnhofstrasse is an experience in itself, with its colorful energy and exquisite environment.

Lake Zurich: Nature lovers can find comfort at the beaches of Lake Zurich. The lake's peaceful waters are suitable for a leisurely boat trip or a quiet afternoon picnic. During the summer months, residents and visitors alike flock here to swim, sunbathe, and enjoy the peacefulness. For a unique view of the city, one may take a boat tour and observe Zurich's skyline framed by the gorgeous Alps.

Uetliberg Mountain: For panoramic views that reach the horizon, a trek up Uetliberg Mountain is needed. Easily accessible from the city center, this mountain provides a choice of paths ideal for various levels of walkers. Once reaching the peak, the view of Zurich and its surrounding surroundings is simply spectacular, especially around dawn or sunset.

Swiss National Museum: Immerse yourself in Switzerland's history and culture at the Swiss National Museum. Housed in a fairytale-like castle, the museum's displays range from medieval antiquities to modern art, offering a thorough picture of the country's development. Intricately created exhibits reflect Switzerland's legacy, making it an instructive and aesthetically pleasing experience.

Kunsthaus Zurich: Art fans will find their home at Kunsthaus Zurich. This art museum features an extraordinary collection of Swiss and international art, encompassing works from the Middle Ages to the present age. Masters like Alberto Giacometti, Marc Chagall, and Vincent van Gogh are among the featured painters. The museum's building itself is a wonder, mixing old and modern flawlessly.

Lindenhof Hill: For a tranquil respite from the metropolitan rush, Lindenhof Hill is a renowned destination. This serene park gives an insight into the city's Roman history and provides a quiet break with its shaded walks, rich gardens, and panoramic vistas. It's a fantastic location to relax, read a book, or just view the city from a fresh perspective.

Zürich Zoo: Families and animal aficionados can find joy at the Zürich Zoo. Home to a broad assortment of animals and environments, including the famed Masoala Rainforest Hall, the zoo provides an informative and exciting experience for visitors of all ages. Conservation initiatives and ecological habitats make this zoo a distinctive attraction.

Detailed guide to must-visit places: Zurich Lake, Uetliberg Mountain, Kunsthaus Zürich, etc.

Zurich, a bustling city set in the heart of Switzerland, provides a lovely combination of natural beauty, cultural richness, and historical importance. From its stunning lakeside vistas to its magnificent mountains and world-class art galleries, Zurich is a treasure mine of experiences waiting to be discovered. In this extensive itinerary, we will take you on a trip through some of the must-visit attractions in Zurich, including Zurich Lake, Uetliberg Mountain, Kunsthaus Zürich, and more.

1. Zurich Lake: A Serene Oasis

Zurich Lake, or "Zürichsee," is a beautiful body of water that charms the city with its natural beauty and calm. With its crystal-clear waters and a magnificent background of the Alps, the lake offers an exquisite setting for both inhabitants and tourists. A leisurely walk along the lakeside promenade gives breathtaking vistas, while boat rides provide a distinct perspective of the city's cityscape. During warmer months, the lake becomes a center for numerous water activities, picnics, and leisure, making it a must-visit location for people seeking a quiet and natural appeal.

2. Uetliberg Mountain: A Panoramic Escape

For a spectacular panoramic view of Zurich and its surroundings, a visit to Uetliberg Mountain is recommended. Accessible through hiking paths or a short train trip, this mountain provides a tranquil getaway into nature. Whether you prefer to climb through beautiful woodlands or take a stroll, the payoff at the peak is undoubtedly worth the effort. The wide panoramas of the city, the lake, and the distant Swiss Alps make a remarkable experience, particularly around dawn or sunset. Uetliberg Mountain appeals to both nature lovers and photography connoisseurs, providing an amazing journey.

3. Kunsthaus Zürich: A Cultural Gem

For art connoisseurs, Kunsthaus Zürich stands as a cultural treasure trove. This famous art museum features an extraordinary collection stretching from the Middle Ages to current masterpieces. Works by Swiss and international artists, including Alberto Giacometti, Marc Chagall, and Vincent van Gogh, decorate its galleries. The museum's numerous exhibits, encompassing painting, sculpture, photography, and more, give a thorough glimpse into the world of art. Whether you're an art enthusiast or just interested, Kunsthaus Zürich ensures a fascinating experience.

4. Old Town (Altstadt): A Glimpse into History

Zurich's Old Town, or Altstadt, is a maze of small lanes, lovely squares, and historical sites. Roaming along its cobblestone streets, you'll see medieval buildings, like the Grossmünster and Fraumünster churches. The Niederdorf neighborhood inside the Old Town is especially bustling, surrounded by stores, cafés, and restaurants. Exploring this neighborhood looks into Zurich's rich history and cultural progress. Don't miss the chance to explore Lindenhof Hill, a historic Roman fortress site, that gives a calm refuge with panoramic views.

5. Bahnhofstrasse: Shopper's Paradise

No visit to Zurich is complete without seeing Bahnhofstrasse, one of the world's most renowned retail avenues. This premium street is lined with luxury boutiques, multinational brands, department stores, and gourmet shops. Even if shopping isn't your major objective, wandering down Bahnhofstrasse looks at the city's rich lifestyle and dynamic commercial environment.

6. Swiss National Museum: Cultural Exploration

Delve into Switzerland's cultural past at the Swiss National Museum, located in a fairytale-like neo-Gothic edifice. The museum's displays depict the country's history, from its early origins to the present times. A broad assortment of objects, including armor, historical fabrics, and traditional crafts, give insight into Swiss identity and growth.

Chapter 6:

Cultural Delights

Nestled in the heart of Switzerland, Zurich stands as a cultural center where heritage smoothly intertwines with contemporary. This charming city, famed for its magnificent landscapes, efficient infrastructure, and booming economy, also features a rich tapestry of cultural pleasures that capture the hearts and minds of tourists and inhabitants alike. From its museums and historical monuments to its dynamic festivals and culinary scene, Zurich offers a broad selection of activities that demonstrate its distinctive combination of legacy and innovation.

Museums and Historical Sites: Preserving the Past

Zurich takes pride in its historical monuments and well-conserved museums that chronicle the tale of its history. The Kunsthaus Zurich, a notable art museum, displays an extraordinary collection of Swiss and foreign art spanning several ages. Its shows vary from Renaissance classics to modern works, presenting an aesthetic journey through time. The Swiss National Museum stands as an architectural jewel, presenting exhibits that illustrate the nation's history and cultural progress. The Old Town (Altstadt) is enchanting with its tiny cobblestone lanes, ancient houses, and the magnificent Grossmünster and Fraumünster churches that have endured for centuries.

Festivals:
Celebrating Diversity

Zurich's cultural calendar is packed with events that celebrate variety and innovation. The Street Parade, an electronic music spectacular, attracts spectators from across the world, covering the city in a riot of colors and rhythms. The Zurich Film Festival highlights worldwide cinematic talent, while the Sechseläuten greets the approach of spring with a horse parade and the burning of the Böögg, a snowman effigy. These events not only amuse but also give a venue for cultural interaction and creative expression.

Performing Arts:
Elegance in Motion

The city's devotion to the performing arts is obvious in its various theaters, opera houses, and concert halls. The Opernhaus Zürich, a world-renowned opera house, performs shows that span classical works and modern ones, reflecting the city's devotion to cultivating creative talent. The Tonhalle Orchestra Zurich mesmerizes listeners with symphonies that resound with heart and expertise. The city's robust theatrical industry varies from experimental performances to classic plays, giving something for every theater aficionado.

Culinary Scene:
A Gastronomic Voyage

Zurich's culinary environment is a combination of history and innovation, bringing food connoisseurs on a gourmet trip. The city's famed cheese fondue, a communal experience of dipping bread into melted cheese, is a treasured Swiss institution. At the same time, enterprising chefs have added a contemporary edge to Swiss cuisine, blending local ingredients with worldwide tastes. The colorful food markets, such as the weekly farmers' market at Bürkliplatz, allow sampling of fresh vegetables and artisanal sweets.

Innovation and Contemporary Art:
Pushing Boundaries

While anchored in history, Zurich thrives on innovation and current expression. The city's emphasis on sustainability and technology is evident in its contemporary architecture and urban design. The Prime Tower, Switzerland's highest skyscraper, stands as a symbol of modernity, while the ETH Zurich, a world-renowned institution, continues to push the frontiers of scientific inquiry. The Löwenbräukunst complex is a center for contemporary art, exhibiting cutting-edge shows that defy traditional standards.

Overview of Zurich's cultural scene: museums, galleries, theaters

Nestled in the heart of Switzerland, Zurich is a lively center of culture and innovation, providing a broad selection of museums, galleries, and theaters that appeal to every creative taste. This gorgeous city, with its rich history and cosmopolitan ambiance, has built a cultural environment that perfectly mixes tradition and modernity.

Museums: Zurich features an astonishing collection of museums that span numerous disciplines, reflecting the city's dedication to conserving its legacy and supporting modern art. The Kunsthaus Zurich, one of the most recognized art museums in Europe, contains a huge collection of artworks stretching from the Middle Ages to the present day, showcasing works by Swiss and international artists. Its extraordinary collection of contemporary art, including paintings by Alberto Giacometti and Marc Chagall, attracts art fans from throughout the globe.

For those curious about Swiss history, the Swiss National Museum provides a thorough trip through the nation's past. Housed in a spectacular fairytale-like castle, the museum shows artifacts, papers, and exhibits that describe Switzerland's cultural progress from ancient times to the present.

Galleries: Zurich's gallery culture is dynamic, giving a venue for budding artists to present their talent alongside famous names. The LUMA Westbau, situated in the Löwenbräukunst complex, is a classic example. It's a contemporary art gallery that often organizes thought-provoking shows, stimulating dialogues about social concerns and current viewpoints.

The PARK Art Space is another notable gallery, noted for its devotion to developing multidisciplinary art genres. It typically offers collaborative shows that transcend conventional artistic boundaries, inviting people to connect with art in new and surprising ways.

Theaters: Zurich's theatrical environment is defined by a dynamic mix of classic and avant-garde acts. The Zurich Opera House serves as a tribute to the city's admiration for historic art forms. With its spectacular architecture and top-tier shows, the opera house provides a world-class experience for fans of opera and ballet.

However, Zurich's theatrical culture stretches beyond the conventional. The Schauspielhaus Zürich is recognized for its unique approach to theater, typically experimenting with unorthodox tales and current subjects. This avant-garde institution pushes the limits of traditional storytelling, drawing a varied audience seeking innovative and thought-provoking experiences.

Cultural Festivals: Zurich's cultural energy is further accentuated by its multitude of festivals that highlight many types of creative expression. The Zurich Film Festival unites directors, actors, and cinephiles from all corners of the world to celebrate the art of filmmaking. It exhibits a combination of worldwide films and local creations, making it a center for cinematic inquiry.

For music fans, the Zurich Street Parade turns the city into a big dance floor, celebrating electronic music and young culture. This yearly event gathers thousands of revelers and is a tribute to Zurich's receptivity to current ideas.

Recommendations for art enthusiasts, music lovers, and theater-goers

Nestled in the heart of Switzerland, Zurich is a city that pulsates with cultural life. Its rich history, stunning scenery, and lively cultural scene make it an appealing destination for art aficionados, music lovers, and theater-goers alike. The Zurich Recommendations include a varied assortment of activities that appeal to these hobbies, delivering a trip into the worlds of art, music, and theater that is remarkable.

Art Enthusiasts: A Canvas of Creativity

For art connoisseurs, Zurich is a treasure trove of creative expression. Begin your trip with the Kunsthaus Zürich, a respected art museum that has a wide collection ranging from medieval to modern art. Admire masterpieces by Swiss and worldwide painters such as Alberto Giacometti, Marc Chagall, and Ferdinand Hodler. The museum's dedication to promoting creativity is reflected in its ever-evolving displays and educational initiatives.

A short journey from the Kunsthaus leads to the Old Town, a tangle of cobblestone alleyways and ancient buildings that breathes history. Galleries like the Helmhaus and the Löwenbräukunst are important visits, presenting modern Swiss and international art. The bustling area of

Zürich-West is an urban canvas decorated with street art and avant-garde galleries, excellent for people seeking cutting-edge innovation.

Music Lovers: Harmonious Melodies

Zurich's music scene seamlessly balances history and innovation. The city's famous Tonhalle Orchestra is a cornerstone of its musical identity, providing classical performances that connect with passion. The Tonhalle itself, a superbly built music venue, enriches the aural experience. Immerse yourself in the works of Mozart, Beethoven, and Strauss, performed by world-class performers.

For individuals oriented towards current sounds, Zurich caters to varied musical interests. The Moods, a jazz club located on the banks of Lake Zurich, pulsates with rhythm and improvisation. World-class jazz artists and upcoming stars visit its stage, giving a one-of-a-kind auditory excursion. The Bogen F, a trendy venue beneath the arches of a railway bridge, is the core of Zurich's alternative music scene. From indie music to electronic sounds, it resonates with the pulses of current inventiveness.

Theater-Goers: The Dramatic Tapestry

The theatrical culture of Zurich crafts tales that touch strongly. The Schauspielhaus Zurich, one of Europe's oldest theaters, enchants spectators with a repertoire ranging from classical plays to avant-garde performances. The impassioned performances by the performers and the finely created sets take theater-goers into enthralling storylines.

For those seeking a more intimate theatrical experience, the Theater Neumarkt delivers experimental and thought-provoking productions that defy norms. The venue's dedication to encouraging innovation is a monument to Zurich's enthusiasm for pushing creative limits. And let's not forget the distinctive art form of cabaret — the Kaufleuten showcases exciting cabaret acts that blend satire, comedy, and social criticism.

Culmination of Passion

The Zurich Recommendations serve as a tribute to the city's devotion to supporting the interests of art aficionados, music lovers, and theater-goers. From the brushstrokes of a painting to the harmonics of a symphony and the passionate emotions on stage, Zurich is a place where creativity flourishes and the human spirit is sparked.

Chapter 7:

Culinary Journey

Zurich, a city recognized for its gorgeous surroundings, lively culture, and rich history, also maintains a prominent position in the world of gastronomic experiences. Embarking on a gastronomic trip around Zurich is equivalent to studying the numerous sides of Swiss food, from classic Alpine tastes to cosmopolitan influences that have merged harmoniously with local customs. This gourmet trip promises to stimulate taste buds, elicit cultural awareness, and create enduring memories.

Zurich's Culinary Tapestry: A Fusion of Tradition and Innovation

The culinary scene in Zurich represents the city's dynamic character, where history meets innovation. Swiss cuisine, frequently inspired by surrounding nations, promotes locally produced foods and workmanship. Traditional foods like fondue and raclette have become iconic, delivering a delicious delight steeped in Swiss Alpine history. These cheese-centric delicacies are best eaten in quaint Swiss chalet-style eateries, encouraging residents and tourists alike to congregate around communal pots of melted cheese and share lovely discussions.

Beyond the conventional, Zurich's culinary environment has accepted foreign influences with open arms. The city's varied population has resulted in a diversity of eateries serving various cuisines, ranging from Italian trattorias to Indian curry houses to contemporary fusion chefs. This beautiful combination of tastes speaks eloquently about Zurich's international nature.

Zurich's Food Markets: A Window to Local Life

A typical approach to immerse oneself in Zurich's gastronomic culture is by visiting its food markets. The lively Bürkliplatz Market exhibits a selection of seasonal fruits, vegetables, cheeses, and artisanal items. Strolling around its booths, one may observe the devotion to quality and sustainability that characterizes Swiss culinary principles. The market not only offers fresh fruit but also gives insight into the everyday life of Zurich's citizens as they assemble to purchase the best foods.

Chocolate & Confections: A Swiss Artform

No journey of Swiss cuisine is complete without indulging in its most recognized export: chocolate. Zurich features a range of world-renowned chocolatiers who continue to improve the technique of converting cocoa beans into delightful delights. Whether it's a visit to the Lindt Chocolate Factory or a walk down the famed Confiserie Sprüngli, where wonderfully smooth pralines and velvety truffles line the shelves, one cannot avoid the appeal of Swiss chocolate-making talent.

Fine Dining and Culinary Innovation

Zurich's culinary adventure continues to its fine dining places, where culinary talent takes center stage. The city has gained a constellation of Michelin stars, showing its capacity to delight even the most discriminating palates. Restaurants like Echo Zürich and The Dolder Grand Restaurant exhibit the ingenuity of local chefs who creatively rework traditional ingredients while keeping a strong sense of Swiss identity.

Celebrating Swiss Wines

A lesser-known part of Zurich's gastronomic journey resides in its vineyards and winemaking tradition. Nestled along the shores of Lake Zurich and in the neighboring hills, vineyards create a diversity of Swiss wines that match the local cuisine. Swiss wines, such as Chasselas and Pinot Noir, exemplify the terroir of the area, delivering a harmonic combination with Zurich's gastronomic pleasures.

Introduction to Swiss cuisine and Zurich's local dishes

Switzerland, tucked in the heart of Europe, is recognized for its magnificent scenery, efficient public transit, and rich cultural history. Among its numerous assets, Swiss food stands out as a pleasant expression of the country's rich history and geographical influences. The food differs from region to region, with each location providing its distinct tastes and ingredients. Zurich, Switzerland's biggest city and cultural center, features a particular culinary culture that eloquently captures the nation's gastronomic character.

Swiss Cuisine: A Blend of Traditions

Swiss cuisine is a perfect combination of influences from nearby nations, such as France, Italy, and Germany, as well as its unique traditions. Due to its landlocked terrain, Swiss cuisine depends primarily on locally obtained ingredients, making it a celebration of seasonal food and artisanal workmanship. One of the most famous Swiss cuisines is fondue, a communal dish where diners dip bread into melted cheese. This custom is rooted in the Alpine regions and is commonly shared in social events, reflecting the Swiss focus on communal meals and conviviality.

Zurich's Gastronomic Tapestry

Zurich, a city recognized for its financial prowess and strong cultural environment, also enjoys a varied gastronomic landscape. The city's cuisine is determined by its historical significance as a commercial center and its closeness to the Swiss Alps. One of Zurich's culinary trademarks is its focus on high-quality ingredients and thorough preparation. This devotion to culinary perfection has won the city a significant position on the world gourmet map.

Zürcher Geschnetzeltes

One of Zurich's most renowned local meals is "Zürcher Geschnetzeltes," a delectable delicacy that comprises sliced veal in a creamy white wine and mushroom sauce. Often served with Rösti, a classic Swiss potato dish, Zürcher Geschnetzeltes exemplifies the city's talent for mixing basic ingredients into an outstanding gourmet experience.

Rösti

Rösti, a delicacy that has become associated with Swiss cuisine, is simply a potato pancake prepared with shredded and fried potatoes. It has modest roots as a farmer's dinner but has blossomed into a national favorite. In Zurich, you'll discover variants that incorporate cheese, bacon, or even apples, displaying the ingenuity of local cooks.

Zürcher Eintopf

For those seeking comfort in a bowl, "Zürcher Eintopf" is a must-try. This substantial beef and vegetable stew represents the Swiss tradition of utilizing local resources to make rich, satisfying meals. The meal has a homey appeal and is a tribute to Zurich's dedication to maintaining culinary tradition.

Zürcher Oberland Specialties

Venturing towards the outskirts of Zurich, you'll meet the Zürcher Oberland area, noted for its gorgeous scenery and wonderful gastronomic choices. Here, you may relish meals like "Zürcher Oberland Mostbröckli," a form of air-dried beef that's thinly sliced and served as an appetizer or part of a charcuterie board. The region's focus on traditional cooking techniques and locally produced foods gives a genuine touch to the culinary experience.

Best restaurants, cafes, and food markets to experience authentic flavors

Nestled inside this busy metropolis are hidden jewels that provide distinct tastes, reflecting the rich cultural legacy and culinary traditions of the area. From quaint cafés to upmarket restaurants and lively food markets, this guide takes you on a scrumptious tour through some of the greatest venues to enjoy Zurich's distinct flavors.

I. Restaurants: Savoring Culinary Excellence

Kronenhalle: Established in 1924, Kronenhalle is a classic restaurant that emanates elegance and heritage. Famous for its sophisticated Swiss cuisine, it includes delicacies like "Zürcher Geschnetzeltes," a veal ragout served with Rösti, embodying the spirit of Swiss comfort food.

Widder Restaurant: Situated inside the Widder Hotel, this restaurant flawlessly merges modern décor with traditional Swiss dishes. It serves a choice of meals employing local products, such as Alpine cheese fondue and seasonal game.

Zeughauskeller: For a hearty experience, Zeughauskeller is the place to go. This rustic cafe is noted for its big quantities of Swiss classics including sausage, sauerkraut, and potato dishes.

II. Cafes: A Taste of Swiss Delights

Café Schober: Transport yourself to a bygone age with Café Schober, a delightful café that goes back to the 19th century. Indulge in scrumptious pastries, Swiss chocolate, and specialty coffees in a lovely, historic environment.

Conditorei Schober: Sister institution to Café Schober, Conditorei Schober provides a selection of homemade pastries, cakes, and chocolates. Their "Luxemburgerli," exquisite macaroon-like pastries, are a must-try.

Café Sprüngli: A Swiss institution since 1836, Café Sprüngli is known for its superb macarons and scrumptious pralines. The sophisticated café atmosphere is great for indulging in a leisurely afternoon tea.

III. Food Markets: A Gastronomic Exploration

Zürich's Farmer's Market: Held on Saturdays, this market is a center for fresh vegetables, artisanal cheeses, cured meats, and freshly baked bread. Engage with local farmers and producers to genuinely appreciate the flavors of the area.

Helvetiaplatz Market: Taking place on Tuesdays and Fridays, this market provides a dynamic mix of foreign and local delicacies. From Swiss cheeses to Mediterranean olives and unique spices, it's a gastronomic feast.

St. Peter's Market: Set against the background of St. Peter's Church, this market offers regional items, like Alpine herbs, homemade sausages, and freshly caught fish from Swiss lakes.

Chapter 8:

Shopping in Zurich

Zurich, the gorgeous Swiss city nestled at the convergence of the Limmat River and Lake Zurich, is famous for its captivating blend of antique beauty and modern sophistication. Beyond its magnificent landscapes and cultural attractions, Zurich presents a distinct shopping experience. With a combination of ancient markets, high-end stores, and contemporary malls, the city caters to a wide range of shopping preferences. From Bahnhofstrasse, one of the world's most recognized retail streets, to the quaint alleyways of the Old Town, Zurich's shopping scene is a magnificent blend of history and luxury.

Bahnhofstrasse: The Epitome of Elegance

At the hub of Zurich's retail allure is Bahnhofstrasse, a boulevard famed for elegance and splendor. Stretching over 1.4 kilometers, this vibrant street is a haven for shoppers seeking distinctive foreign brands and high-end Swiss things. Here, you'll find flagship stores of worldwide fashion businesses, prominent watchmakers, and jewelry designers, making it a refuge for anyone with a penchant for luxury.

Beyond its variety of luxury boutiques, Bahnhofstrasse has architectural beauty and spectacular panoramas. The street is surrounded by old buildings, stunning facades, and attractive cafés, creating an experience that extends beyond shopping. During the holiday season, Bahnhofstrasse transforms into a winter wonderland with shimmering lights and enticing decorations, providing an amazing setting for Christmas shoppers.

Old Town: A Journey Through Time

For a more true and traditional shopping experience, a visit to Zurich's Old Town is a must. The narrow meandering lanes of Niederdorf and Oberdorf emanate historical charm and are studded with boutique stores, art galleries, and local artisan companies. The Old Town's brilliant vitality and unique character create an ambiance that transports travelers back in time while presenting a diverse array of shopping opportunities.

Markets such as the Rosenhof Market and the weekly Flohmarkt Kanzlei flea market offer a place for local artisans and businesses to showcase their wares. Visitors may explore artisan jewelry, textiles, antiques, and unusual souvenirs, all while immersing themselves in the rich culture and history of Zurich.

Swiss Quality and Craftsmanship

Zurich's shopping experience extends beyond standard retail establishments. Traditional Swiss workmanship is on full exhibit, allowing visitors to take home a piece of Switzerland's cultural legacy. Watch aficionados will find themselves in horological heaven because Zurich is a hub for renowned watchmakers, offering watches that are both utilitarian and gorgeous pieces of art.

Swiss chocolate and sweets also play a vital position in Zurich's retail industry. Chocolatiers like Sprüngli and Läderach give a range of exquisite delights, making it the ideal spot to indulge in some of the greatest chocolate in the world.

Modern Shopping Complexes

In addition to its historical attraction, Zurich has modern shopping complexes that cater to all inclinations. The completely remodeled

Jelmoli, Switzerland's greatest luxury department store, delivers a diverse range of international and local brands under one roof. The Sihlcity Mall includes a variety of shopping, dining, and entertainment activities in a contemporary atmosphere.

Sustainable Shopping

Zurich's attention to sustainability is also evident in its retail landscape. Eco-conscious buyers may explore a range of businesses that promote ethical processes and environmentally beneficial merchandise. From things manufactured with sustainable materials to zero-waste merchants, the city encourages responsible shopping.

Guide to retail areas and streets

With a blend of elegant stores, beautiful street markets, and eccentric retail zones, Zurich presents an unequaled shopping experience that caters to all interests and inclinations. In this tour, we will take a closer look at some of Zurich's most-known retail districts and streets, showcasing the diversity and creativity that make each neighborhood a shopping paradise.

Bahnhofstrasse: At the hub of Zurich's retail sector lies the iconic Bahnhofstrasse. This legendary street is usually regarded to be one of the world's most exclusive shopping lanes, featuring a range of high-end boutiques, luxury brands, and worldwide names. From apparel to jewelry, watches, and cosmetics, Bahnhofstrasse delivers a refined shopping experience that appeals to the discerning shopper. The Boulevard is also decorated with exquisite cafés and restaurants, delivering a fantastic combination of retail therapy and relaxation.

Niederdorf: For a more distinctive and bohemian shopping experience, Niederdorf is the place to go. This old neighborhood is famous for its picturesque cobblestone lanes, art galleries, and local boutiques. Here, purchasers may pursue a choice of unique things, including artisan crafts, vintage fashion, and antiques. Niederdorf also offers a booming nightlife scene, making it an ideal location for individuals looking to shop during the day and indulge in entertainment at night.

Zurich-West: Once an industrial district, Zurich-West has turned into a stylish zone with a blend of current retail concepts and artistic flair. This district is notable for its converted warehouses, which now accommodate a range of design shops, concept businesses, and art galleries. Zurich-West is a hotbed for innovation, bringing both local designers and international enterprises that create inventive and cutting-edge items. From fashion to interior design, Zurich-West caters to shoppers seeking a more contemporary shopping experience.

Strehlgasse: Nestled within Zurich's Old Town, Strehlgasse gives a lovely shopping experience redolent of traditional Swiss architecture. This lovely street is home to a range of handmade stores, boutique booksellers, and local designers. Shoppers may find Swiss-made crafts, chocolates, textiles, and other genuine Swiss things. Strehlgasse's intimate ambiance and historical surroundings make it an interesting site for those looking to immerse themselves in Zurich's past.

Viadukt: Viadukt is a retail venue that effectively mixes modernity with tradition. Located under the arches of an ancient railway viaduct, this area contains a mix of boutiques, concept stores, and specialist businesses. Here, consumers may discover a blend of fashion, home décor, gourmet food, and design goods. Viadukt also features a lively market on Saturdays, when local sellers supply fresh vegetables, artisanal products, and crafts.

Sihlcity: For a comprehensive shopping experience that also includes entertainment and restaurants, Sihlcity is the ideal choice. This shopping area features a broad range of enterprises, from apparel shops to electronics, and even a multi-screen cinema. Sihlcity's architecture includes a blend of modern flair and sustainability, giving a welcome location for retail connoisseurs and families alike.

Tips for finding Swiss watches, chocolates, clothing, and souvenirs

Zurich, the magnificent Swiss city located in the Alps, is a treasure trove of beauty and culture. Renowned for its impeccable craftsmanship, tasty chocolates, sophisticated design, and distinctive souvenirs, Zurich promises a shopping experience unlike any other. This book will provide crucial insights on navigating Zurich's hectic landscape to identify the finest Swiss watches, chocolates, fashion items, and souvenirs, guaranteeing you carry home a part of the city's spirit.

Swiss Watches:

Research Brands: Switzerland is famous for watchmaker excellence. Before starting your watch-hunting expedition, review renowned Swiss watch brands including Rolex, Patek Philippe, and Omega. Understanding the brand's history, craftsmanship, and unique styles will help you make an informed decision.

Visit Bahnhofstrasse: Bahnhofstrasse is a must-visit for watch lovers. This historic retail strip is lined with luxury businesses and authorized dealers providing a spectacular array of Swiss watches. Take your time to explore various companies and compare styles, designs, and price ranges.

Expert Advice: Seek guidance from skilled salespeople who can provide insights into the subtle details of each watch. They may aid you grasp the craftsmanship, movement sorts, and materials employed, permitting you to create a well-informed pick.

Chocolates:

Explore Confiserie Shops: Swiss chocolate is recognized worldwide for its quality and flavor. Wander through old confidence shops like Sprüngli or Läderach, where you can indulge in a range of pralines, truffles, and chocolate bars.

Artisanal Chocolate Enterprises: Venture beyond the well-known brands to locate small artisanal chocolate businesses. These hidden treasures give unexpected taste combinations, handcrafted chocolates, and a personalized touch that you won't find anyplace.

Taste Testing: Many chocolate establishments give free samples, allowing you to explore numerous varieties before making a purchase. Don't hesitate to ask the staff for suggestions based on your likes.

Fashion:

Visit Luxury Boutiques: Zurich's Bahnhofstrasse is a fashion lover's delight. Explore high-end boutiques and flagship stores of renowned luxury brands to unearth the newest fashion trends and timeless goods.

Support Local Designers: Zurich-West is home to a vibrant fashion sector, with local designers and concept firms. Discover unusual objects that demonstrate Swiss craftsmanship and innovation.

Quality Over Quantity: When shopping for stylish products, pick quality over quantity. Swiss fashion is famous for its attention to detail and great materials, so invest in products that will endure the test of time.

Souvenirs:

Traditional Swiss presents: Look for gifts that embody Swiss culture, such as skillfully made cowbells, hand-carved wooden figurines, and Swiss army knives. These things are not only essential but also demonstrate Swiss craftsmanship.

Artisan Workshops: Seek out artisan workshops where you may get handmade pottery, textiles, and other products directly from the creators. This not only aids local crafters but also ensures the authenticity of your souvenirs.

Local Markets: Visit local markets like the one at Viadukt to find a diverse choice of souvenirs, including handmade crafts, gourmet delights, and unique gifts that express the character of Zurich.

Chapter 9:

Outdoor Adventures

Nestled in the heart of Switzerland, Zurich is recognized for its gorgeous surroundings, vibrant metropolitan life, and a unique combination of modernism and history. Beyond the city's attractive streets and cultural attractions, lies an outdoor enthusiast's heaven - Zurich Outdoor Adventures. This is not simply a corporation or an activity center; it's a doorway to experience the breathtaking natural beauty and adrenaline activities that the area has to offer.

The Natural Playground:

Zurich Outdoor Adventures capitalizes on the region's varied landscape, which extends from the tranquil beaches of Lake Zurich to the spectacular peaks of the Swiss Alps. The landscapes provide a plethora of chances for outdoor lovers of all levels, whether they're seeking a peaceful walk along the lakeside promenades or an adrenaline-pumping mountain adventure.

Activities Galore:

The array of activities provided by Zurich Outdoor Adventures is astounding. For those who prefer water-based exploits, kayaking and paddleboarding on Lake Zurich give a unique view of the city's cityscape. Adventurous souls may try their mettle with rock climbing and rappelling in the neighboring mountains, while hiking paths appeal to both novices and experienced hikers. During winter, skiing and snowboarding in adjacent resorts convert the landscape into a snowy paradise.

Guided Expeditions:

What sets Zurich Outdoor Adventures unique is its focus on offering guided adventures led by seasoned specialists. These guides are not only well-versed in outdoor safety but also share a strong appreciation for the environment and local culture. They guarantee that participants not only experience exhilarating activities but also receive insights into the area's history, ecology, and biodiversity.

Sustainability and Ecotourism:

Zurich Outdoor Adventures lays a major focus on sustainable techniques and responsible ecotourism. This devotion guarantees that the beauty of the natural environment stays maintained for future generations. Participants are informed about

Leave No Trace principles and are urged to respect the ecosystems they visit.

Cultural Immersion:

Beyond the physical activities, Zurich Outdoor Adventures also offers opportunities for cultural immersion. Guided trips could include visits to picturesque mountain communities, cheese-making demonstrations, and encounters with local artists. This unique combination of outdoor activity and cultural events provides participants with a full knowledge of the area.

Accessibility and Inclusivity:

One of the company's noteworthy aspects is its focus to make outdoor excursions accessible to a broad spectrum of individuals. Tailored experiences are developed for families, individuals, and groups, ensuring that everyone can participate and appreciate the beauty of the Swiss outdoors.

Creating Lasting Memories:

Zurich Outdoor Adventures provides more than simple activities; it produces enduring experiences. The breathtaking sunsets viewed from mountain tops, the camaraderie developed on group treks, and the pleasure of defeating personal difficulties all combine into an experience that participants take with them long after they've returned home.

Exploring outdoor activities: hiking, biking, boating

Nestled in the heart of Switzerland, Zurich is a city recognized for its balanced combination of contemporary urbanity and pure natural settings. Beyond the busy streets and cultural attractions is a world of outdoor experiences waiting to be explored.

From the peaceful beaches of Lake Zurich to the rocky trails of the neighboring Alps, this dynamic city provides an abundance of outdoor activities that appeal to explorers of all abilities. In this study, we dig into the joy of hiking, bicycling, and boating, exploring the riches that Zurich's environment has to offer.

Hiking Escapades:

Zurich's gorgeous surroundings make it a perfect location for trekking aficionados. The city is graced with a large network of well-maintained trails that weave through lush woods, quiet meadows, and steep ascents that reward hikers with spectacular panoramic vistas. Whether you're seeking a leisurely walk or a difficult mountain trip, Zurich's hiking alternatives suit diverse inclinations.

One of the most recognizable hikes is the Uetliberg Mountain trail. Rising immediately west of Zurich, Uetliberg provides a choice of trails appropriate for families, casual hikers, and keen trekkers alike. The route climbs to a vantage point atop the mountain, offering hikers an awe-inspiring view over the city, Lake Zurich, and the distant Alps. The trail's accessibility through public transit makes it a popular alternative for people wishing to escape the urban bustle without traveling too far.

Biking Adventures:

For bicycle lovers, Zurich's riding paths offer an enjoyable opportunity to experience the region's different landscapes. From quiet lakeside routes to tough mountain pathways, motorcyclists may immerse themselves in the natural splendor while experiencing the excitement of two-wheeled discovery.

The Lake Zurich Cycling Path is a highlight, providing a picturesque path that travels beside the shimmering waters of the lake. Cyclists may bike through picturesque towns, pass past historic buildings, and halt at lakeside cafés to absorb in the peacefulness. More experienced cyclists could travel into the adjacent hills and mountains, facing hard terrain that rewards their efforts with spectacular panoramas.

Boating Serenity:

Lake Zurich provides both a recreational playground and a tranquil getaway from the metropolitan bustle. Boating lovers may participate in a variety of water-based sports that vary from peaceful paddleboarding to more daring kayaking and sailing.

Renting a rowboat or a pedal boat gives a relaxing opportunity to traverse the lake's clean waters while enjoying unimpeded views of the surrounding scenery. Those wanting a more guided experience may take boat trips that give historical insights into

Zurich's coastline and the cultural importance of the lake.

Connecting with Nature and Culture:

Beyond the physical activities, experiencing Zurich's outdoors gives a unique chance to engage with both nature and local culture. The outdoor areas are connected with the city's rich history, establishing a symbiotic interaction between the urban and natural worlds.

Picnicking by the lakeside, enjoying a refreshing bath in the clear waters, or just absorbing the calm of the surroundings offers a deep feeling of refreshment. Additionally, the outdoor areas regularly feature cultural activities, such as open-air concerts and art displays, perfectly integrating relaxation with cultural enrichment.

Inclusivity and Sustainability:

Zurich's dedication to inclusion and sustainability is reflected in its approach to outdoor activities. The city lays a high focus on protecting and preserving its natural beauty, fostering responsible outdoor habits that guarantee the environment stays pure for generations to come. Trails and walkways are well-marked, amenities are maintained, and explanatory signs teach visitors about the necessity of eco-friendly conduct.

Details about surrounding nature reserves and parks

Zurich, a city noted for its active urban life and spectacular architecture, also features a treasure trove of neighboring natural reserves and parks that give a tranquil respite from the rush and bustle of daily life. These verdant sanctuaries give a chance for both inhabitants and tourists to reconnect with nature, immerse themselves in peace, and engage in outdoor sports. In this excursion, we dig into the intricacies of some of the most appealing natural reserves and parks that beautify the region of Zurich.

1. Zurich Zoo and Masoala Rainforest Hall: While not a typical nature reserve, the Zurich Zoo stands as a unique conservation project that brings visitors closer to the beauties of the natural world. The Masoala Rainforest Hall is a unique attraction, where visitors may experience a reconstructed Madagascar rainforest habitat. The entire experience allows for interactions with various species, rich flora, and flowing waterfalls, all while fostering education and understanding about the necessity of protecting these vulnerable settings.

2. Sihlwald Forest Nature Reserve: Just a short distance from the city center, the Sihlwald Forest Nature Reserve stands as a refuge of biodiversity and calm. This natural forest provides a network of well-maintained hiking routes that run among old trees, wildflower meadows, and the peaceful sounds of the Sihl River. The reserve's dedication to sustainability and protection is clear, making it a great destination for nature lovers, birdwatchers, and anybody seeking tranquility in the embrace of pristine wilderness.

3. Türlersee Nature Reserve: Situated on the outskirts of Zurich, the Türlersee Nature Reserve has a lovely lake surrounded by lush trees and undulating hills. The pristine waters of the lake attract tourists to indulge in boating, fishing, and picnics, while the surrounding trails give sufficient chances for strolls and vigorous treks. The reserve's pastoral attractiveness makes it a favorite place for families, couples, and people seeking a calm respite from the city's noise.

4. Katzensee Nature Reserve: Nestled inside the city borders, the Katzensee

Nature Reserve is a tribute to Zurich's determination to protect urban green areas. This tiny but important reserve is home to a tranquil lake, marshes, and meadows that offer a shelter for a diversity of plant and animal species. Birdwatchers will find joy in viewing a broad assortment of feathered occupants, and the well-maintained walking routes enable visitors to explore the natural beauty at their speed.

5. Lindenhof Park: Transitioning from traditional natural reserves to urban green areas, Lindenhof Park maintains historical importance with its natural attractiveness. This historic Roman hilltop park gives panoramic views of the city and the Limmat River. It serves as a serene refuge where tourists may rest on its grassy lawns, surrounded by the vestiges of Roman fortifications and a tranquil environment. Lindenhof Park is not just a testimony to Zurich's rich history but also a testament to the city's dedication to conserving green areas despite urban expansion.

6. Irchelpark: Situated near the University of Zurich, Irchelpark elegantly integrates flora with education. This large park contains a range of plant types, botanical gardens, and peaceful ponds. Visitors may enjoy strolls, picnics, or just soak in the calm of the surroundings. Irchelpark's botanical garden, with its chosen collection of plants from throughout the globe, offers a chance for both rest and study.

Chapter 10.

Day Trips from Zurich

Nestled in the heart of Europe, Switzerland is recognized for its gorgeous scenery, charming towns, and bustling cities. Zurich, the biggest city in the country, provides a good starting place for discovering the numerous interesting sites that lay only a short drive away. This article digs into some of the most intriguing day excursions from Zurich, providing a peek into the spectacular natural beauty and rich cultural legacy that Switzerland has to offer.

Lucerne: Located only an hour's train journey from Zurich, Lucerne is a lovely city that draws guests with its ancient architecture, tranquil lakeside setting, and stunning mountain vistas. The renowned Kapellbrücke (Chapel Bridge) and Water

Tower are among the city's icons, while a walk along the beaches of Lake Lucerne provides a calm getaway. Don't miss the opportunity to enjoy a boat trip on the lake and ride the world's steepest cogwheel train up Mount Pilatus for magnificent sights.

Interlaken: Nestled between Lake Thun and Lake Brienz, Interlaken is heaven for adventure seekers. This gorgeous town provides a wealth of adrenaline-pumping sports, from paragliding and skydiving to hiking and skiing, depending on the season. With its central position, Interlaken provides a gateway to the Jungfrau area, where you may go to the "Top of Europe" by riding the Jungfrau Railway to Jungfraujoch, the highest railway station in Europe.

Bern: The Swiss capital, Bern, features a well-preserved medieval old town that is a UNESCO World Heritage site. Its cobblestone streets, clock tower, and Zytglogge (Clock Tower) are just a few of the architectural jewels that give an insight into the country's past. Bear Park, Rosengarten (Rose Garden), and the Federal Palace are additional must-visit sites. Bern's calm atmosphere and cultural diversity make it a great day excursion from Zurich.

Rhine Falls: For a natural sight, a visit to the Rhine Falls is a must. Just a short train ride from Zurich, these falls are the biggest in Europe and give a stunning picture as the tremendous waves flow down the rocks. Visitors may take a boat trip to go up close to the falls or explore the walking paths that give numerous vantage points for appreciating this awe-inspiring natural phenomenon.

Mount Titlis: Another wonderful alpine experience awaits at Mount Titlis. Accessible via a mix of railways, cable cars, and a revolving gondola, this attraction provides a unique experience. The climb to the peak includes stunning panoramas of glaciers, rocky terrain, and the iconic Titlis Cliff Walk — Europe's highest suspension bridge. A feature is a permanently snowy landscape, allowing for snow activities even in the summer months.

Zurich Oberland: If you're hoping to discover the lesser-known treasures around Zurich, the Zurich Oberland area is a hidden treasure. This region is distinguished by undulating hills, lovely towns, and magnificent scenery. A visit to the Camden area provides tranquil hiking paths, while the town of Einsiedeln is home to a beautiful baroque-style Benedictine abbey.

Excursions to local attractions: Lucerne, Bern, Rhine Falls, etc.

Switzerland, with its awe-inspiring scenery, rich cultural history, and lovely towns, draws people from across the globe to experience its riches. Nestled amid this tapestry of splendor are numerous surrounding destinations that make for great outings. From the calm beaches of Lake Lucerne to the medieval alleys of Bern, and the majestic cascade of the Rhine Falls, this essay digs into the fascination of these extraordinary sites.

Lucerne: Enchanting Lakefront Beauty

Situated only a stone's throw away from Zurich, Lucerne is a postcard-perfect city that symbolizes the classic Swiss charm. Its landmark Kapellbrücke, decked with beautiful flowers, bridges the Reuss River, bringing tourists into a labyrinth of cobblestone lanes dotted with ancient buildings. As you explore the Old Town, find secret squares, centuries-old buildings, and pleasant cafés. Lucerne's lakeside position adds to its charm, with the crystal-clear waters of Lake Lucerne reflecting the surrounding snow-capped Alps. A leisurely boat trip on the lake gives a unique view of the city's attractiveness and the stunning mountains that surround it.

Bern: Timeless Elegance and Heritage

Switzerland's capital city, Bern, takes tourists back in time with its immaculately maintained medieval buildings and a calm pace of life. The Zytglogge, a 13th-century clock tower, mesmerizes tourists with its elaborate astronomical clock and hourly mechanical spectacle. The Bern Minster, a stunning Gothic cathedral, gives panoramic views of the city from its tower. The Federal Palace, housing the Swiss government, is a testimony to Bern's importance in the country's history. The lovely arcades that flank the streets are great for shopping and eating Swiss cuisine. Bern's unique combination of history and contemporary produces an ambiance that is both charming and hospitable.

Rhine Falls: Nature's Majestic Symphony

A short ride from Zurich, the Rhine Falls gives a vision of nature's majesty. The thunderous rivers flow over steep rocks, producing a symphony of sound and a foggy haze that envelops the surroundings. A boat ride puts you tantalizingly near the falls, delivering an awe-inspiring experience as you feel the strength of the water under you. A network of well-maintained walkways and views enables visitors to see the falls from numerous perspectives, conveying the tremendous magnitude of this European beauty. A visit to the adjacent Schloss Laufen lends historical context to the environment, with its medieval castle overlooking the falls.

Lucerne to Interlaken: The Scenic Journey

En route from Lucerne to Interlaken lies an exquisite trip that encapsulates Switzerland's breathtaking grandeur. The GoldenPass Line brings you through verdant valleys, picturesque towns, and meadows filled with Swiss chalets. The tour concludes at Interlaken, a haven for adventure aficionados. Nestled between Lake Thun and Lake Brienz, Interlaken provides sports like paragliding, skydiving, and hiking. From here, you may also begin on a spectacular trek to Jungfraujoch, the "Top of Europe," giving panoramic views of the Alps.

Exploring the Uncharted: Lesser-Known Gems

Beyond the well-trodden roads, Switzerland's lesser-known sites provide an intimate peek into its culture and scenery. Einsiedeln, noted for its awe-inspiring Benedictine abbey, highlights the country's spiritual legacy against a background of serene landscape. A visit to Amden shows undulating hills and tranquil hiking routes that lead to beautiful panoramas. These eccentric sites enable tourists to interact with Switzerland on a more intimate level, away from the tourist throng.

How to plan day excursions and what to anticipate

Embarking on a day trip is an amazing opportunity to escape routine and discover new vistas, all within a single day. Whether you're seeking a calm retreat, an adventure-filled excursion, or a cultural immersion, thorough preparation and establishing realistic expectations are crucial to having a successful and fulfilling trip. This guide will take you through the processes of organizing day excursions and give insights into what you may anticipate along the route.

Planning Day Trips:

place Selection: Start by picking a place that corresponds with your interests and travel style. Consider considerations such as distance, journey duration, available transit alternatives, and the sights or activities you intend to visit.

Research: Dive into research to collect knowledge about the selected place. Look into the key attractions, historical sites, natural features, local cuisine, and any special events that could be occurring on the day of your trip. Online travel guides, websites, and travel forums may give helpful information.

plan Creation: Design a preliminary plan that covers the must-visit locations and a flexible time frame. Be careful of opening hours, guided tours, and possible peak hours to avoid crowds. Allow some spare time for unexpected discoveries and relaxation.

Transportation: Decide on the method of transportation that matches your route. Whether it's via rail, bus, automobile, or a combination, ensure you have a thorough awareness of timetables, routes, and possible delays. Booking tickets in advance might save you time and guarantee smoother travel.

Packing basics: Depending on your location and intended activities, bring basics such as comfortable walking shoes, weather-appropriate clothes, sunscreen, a map or navigation software, a fully charged phone, and any required identification or tickets.

Meals and Snacks: Research meal alternatives at your destination and carry snacks for the ride. Trying local food is part of the experience, so consider arranging reservations if required. Stay hydrated throughout the day to keep your energy levels up.

Budgeting: Set a budget for the day trip, including transportation, admission fees, lunch, and any souvenirs. Having a clear budget can help you manage expenditures and make the most of your day without worrying about overpaying.

Expectations for Day Trips:

Time Management: Day excursions are all about maximizing your time, therefore smart time management is key. Stick to your plan as precisely as possible to ensure you cover the key attractions. However, be open to spontaneity and give opportunities for unanticipated diversions.

Crowds and Peak Hours: Popular attractions could have more foot traffic, particularly during weekends and holidays. Plan to visit these locations early in the day or later in the afternoon to escape the greatest crowds.

Weather Considerations: Weather may dramatically affect your day travel experience. Check the weather prediction in advance and dress appropriately. Be prepared for variations in weather conditions, particularly if your trip includes outdoor activities.

Flexibility and Unexpected Delights: While preparation is crucial, be prepared to adjust if things don't go precisely as planned. Unexpected discoveries and diversions frequently lead to some of the most unforgettable moments.

Physical and Mental Preparedness: Day excursions may be physically taxing, particularly if they entail a lot of walking or outdoor activities. Ensure you're physically prepared by wearing suitable footwear and taking breaks as required. Stay psychologically prepared for a long day of research and probable adjustments.

Embrace the Experience: Keep in mind that day excursions are designed to be pleasurable and restorative. Embrace the experience, absorb the sights and sounds, and record moments to cherish later.

Chapter 11:

Nightlife and Entertainment

Zurich, a lovely city set in the heart of Switzerland, is recognized not just for its breathtaking landscapes and ancient architecture but also for its active nightlife and numerous entertainment choices. From frenetic clubs to quaint theaters, Zurich's nightlife scene easily integrates the city's rich cultural legacy with current trends, making it a magnet for residents and visitors alike seeking a dynamic and unique experience.

Diverse gastronomic Delights: The city's entertainment tapestry starts with its gastronomic sector. As the sun sets, Zurich's countless restaurants, cafés, and food markets come to life, presenting a diversity of exotic cuisines that appeal to every appetite. Whether you're in the mood for classic Swiss fondue, delicious Italian pasta, or inventive fusion cuisine, Zurich's culinary scene offers it all. The blend of excellent food and a welcoming setting sets the tone for a riveting evening ahead.

Spectacular Theatrical Performances: For those wanting a touch of elegance, Zurich's theaters offer an excellent retreat. The city features several theaters, both big and small, featuring a spectrum of performances from classical plays to avant-garde shows. The famous Zurich Opera House stands as a peak of artistic quality, featuring world-class operas, ballets, and symphonic concerts. Attending a play at one of Zurich's theaters is a chance to immerse oneself in the city's cultural legacy and creative genius.

Lively Nightclubs and Bars: As the night deepens, Zurich changes into a sanctuary for night owls with its booming nightlife scene. The city is dotted with a myriad of pubs, clubs, and lounges that cater to varied musical preferences. Whether you're a lover of throbbing techno sounds, live jazz groups, or soothing acoustic performances, Zurich's nightlife offers a broad range of musical experiences. The Langstrasse quarter is especially noted for its active nightlife, with a combination of pubs, clubs, and street food booths that keep the spirit alive into the early hours.

Lake Zurich's Magnetic Charm: One of the most captivating parts of Zurich's nightlife is the city's closeness to Lake Zurich. The glistening waters of the lake create a picturesque background for diverse nocturnal activities. During the summer months, the lake's banks come alive with open-air concerts, lakeside picnics, and tranquil boat excursions. As the moonlight dances across the lake, residents and tourists congregate to relish the tranquil environment that Lake Zurich provides.

Festivals & Events: Zurich's calendar is overflowing with festivals and events that bring an additional layer of excitement to the city's nightlife. The Street Parade, an annual electronic dance music event, pulls thousands of revelers from across the globe to the streets of Zurich, creating an exciting environment. The Zurich Film Festival celebrates the art of cinema and draws famous directors, actors, and film aficionados, delivering a unique combination of beauty and culture.

Embracing Tradition with a Modern Twist: What sets Zurich's nightlife different is its ability to effortlessly integrate tradition with modernity. Historic locations frequently undergo imaginative renovations, holding modern events that connect with both residents and tourists. This blend of old and modern is reflected by the city's bustling club culture, where industrial warehouses are turned into cutting-edge dance places, producing an ambiance that is both genuine and trendsetting.

Overview of Zurich's thriving nightlife: pubs, clubs, live music

Nestled among the gorgeous Swiss landscapes, Zurich stands as a beacon of culture, innovation, and nightlife excitement. As the sun sets behind the Alps, the city's dynamic nightlife wakes, providing a broad choice of events for both inhabitants and tourists. From refined pubs to throbbing clubs and soul-stirring live music venues, Zurich's nightlife culture offers a voyage across an exhilarating spectrum of entertainment.

Bars: Where Elegance Meets Relaxation

Zurich's evening experience generally starts in its attractive bars, each with its distinct ambiance and character. Whether you need a calm spot to relax or a bustling setting to kick-start your night, the city provides an incredible choice of possibilities.

Jules Verne Panoramabar: Perched atop the Haus Ober restaurant, this bar boasts panoramic views of the city's cityscape and Lake Zurich. Sip on carefully made cocktails while basking in the spectacular vistas, making it a great setting for an elegant precursor to the night.

Old Crow: Infused with a touch of classic Americana, Old Crow draws consumers with its rustic appeal and well-chosen range of spirits. The bar's trademark drinks pay respect to traditional formulas while adding a contemporary touch, making it a must-visit for cocktail connoisseurs.

Tales Bar: Enveloped in an air of mysticism, Tales Bar presents an extensive menu of excellent drinks inspired by the art of storytelling. With mixologists as talented narrators, each cocktail comes with a narrative that compliments its tastes, providing an immersive experience for the senses.

Clubs: Pulsating Heartbeats of the Night

When the need to dance takes over, Zurich's bustling club scene is ready to sweep you off your feet. These venues provide a dynamic combination of music, energy, and companionship, making them crucial destinations for people wishing to immerse themselves in rhythm.

Hive: Known for its cutting-edge electronic music scene, Hive serves as a magnet for techno and house fans. With its state-of-the-art music system and immersive lighting design, the club's subterranean ambiance offers an unrivaled setting for nighttime celebrations.

Kaufleuten: Embracing both historical and modern elements, Kaufleuten is a multi-faceted entertainment destination. By day, it's a classy restaurant and bar; by night, it turns into a high-energy club featuring live DJ performances and a varied clientele.

Mascotte: Blending a bit of nostalgic charm with new sounds, Mascotte has been a fixture of Zurich's nightlife for decades. This tiny club provides live music events spanning genres from rock and pop to techno, assuring a fantastic night for music fans.

Live Music Venues: Harmonic Chronicles Unfold

For those who enjoy their pleasure in live soundscapes, Zurich's live music venues serve a broad range of preferences. From soul-stirring melodies to foot-stomping rhythms, these stages reverberate with the heartbeats of artists and listeners alike.

Moods Jazz Club: Reverberating with the soulful sounds of jazz, Moods Jazz Club is a paradise for fans of improvisation and musical innovation. With its compact atmosphere and famous musicians gracing the stage, it delivers an immersive experience for music aficionados.

Kinski: A melting pot of musical styles, Kinski is a flexible live music venue that attracts indie bands, singer-songwriters, and experimental artists. Its diversified programming guarantees that there's something for everyone, making it a meeting location for the city's unique music scene.

EXIL: Celebrating the underground music scene, EXIL showcases an assortment of live performances spanning hip-hop, electronic, and alternative genres. Its devotion to young artists and varied lineups makes it a destination for finding the next great thing in music.

Recommendations for a good evening out

In the hurry and bustle of daily life, there's nothing quite like heading out for a fun evening to relax, mingle, and make lasting memories. Whether you're planning a night out with pals, a romantic escapade, or a solitary trip, the choices are unlimited. From eating experiences to entertainment possibilities, here are some tips to help you construct a memorable and pleasurable evening.

Culinary Adventures: Savoring Every Bite

Begin your evening by engaging in a fantastic gastronomic excursion. Choose a restaurant that corresponds with your interests, whether it's a comfortable café, a trendy bistro, or unusual dining. Here's how to make the most of your eating experience:

Try Something New: Opt for a food you've never experienced before. Exploring diverse tastes and ingredients may bring an air of excitement to your evening.

Tasting Menus: Many restaurants offer tasting menus, enabling you to try a variety of foods in smaller servings. This is a terrific way to taste a varied variety of flavors in one meal.

Food Markets & Street Food: If you're in a city renowned for its food markets or street food culture, try taking a walk around these colorful areas. You may enjoy local specialties and engage with sellers, bringing a sense of authenticity to your evening.

Cooking Classes: If you're searching for a hands-on experience, try attending a cooking class with friends or your spouse.

Learning to create a new meal may be both informative and amusing.

Cultural Experiences: Nurturing the Mind and Soul

After a hearty dinner, it's time to fuel your mind and spirit with cultural activities. These may involve exploring art, music, drama, and more:

Art Galleries and Museums: Visit local art galleries or museums to immerse yourself in creativity and cultural enrichment. Many towns provide nighttime exhibits and other events that lend an added layer of charm to the experience.

Live Performances: Attend a live music concert, theater play, or dance performance. The excitement of a live event and the connection with the artists may leave a lasting imprint.

Film Screenings: Check if any film festivals or special screenings are going on in your region. Watching a thought-provoking or amusing film might be a terrific way to spend your evening.

Historical Tours: If you're interested in history, try attending a guided historical tour of your city. Discover secret tales, places, and anecdotes that you may not have known before.

Entertainment Options: Laughter and Amusement

When it comes to entertainment, there's something for everyone. Whether you're in the mood for humor, excitement, or relaxation, these tips may help:

Comedy Clubs: A night of laughing may do wonders for your mood. Check out local comedy clubs or stand-up comedy acts for a dose of fun.

Arcades and Game Nights: Engage in some friendly rivalry by visiting an arcade or organizing a game night with friends. Whether it's video games, board games, or trivia, you're guaranteed to have fun.

Outdoor Activities: Depending on the season, outdoor activities like mini-golf, picnics, or stargazing may be a unique and entertaining way to spend your evening.

Escape Rooms: Challenge your problem-solving talents by engaging in an escape room experience. It's a fun and interesting exercise that fosters collaboration and innovation.

Strolling and Relaxation: Nature's Tranquil Escape

If you're wanting a more calm and thoughtful evening, try spending time outdoors:

Evening Walks: Take a leisurely walk in a park, along a waterfront, or in a botanical garden. The calm environment may be immensely rejuvenating.

Sunset Viewing: Find a position with a panoramic view of the sunset. Whether it's a hill, a rooftop bar, or a beach, watching the sun sink below the horizon can be a contemplative and beautiful experience.

Boat Rides: If you're near a body of water, try taking a boat trip in the evening. Whether it's a rowboat, paddleboat, or a leisurely cruise, the water may bring a feeling of peace.

Outdoor Yoga or Meditation: Many cities provide outdoor yoga or meditation classes throughout the evening. Joining one of these workshops might help you relax and focus on yourself.

Chapter 12:

Family-Friendly Zurich

Zurich, the bustling and culturally diverse city located at the heart of Switzerland, has gained a reputation for its gorgeous landscapes, ancient architecture, and economic success. However, beyond its financial center and urban attractions, Zurich provides a multitude of family-friendly events that appeal to tourists of all ages. From gorgeous parks and engaging museums to interactive activities and gastronomic pleasures, this attractive city flawlessly merges the best of both worlds - a busy metropolitan setting with a loving family-oriented ambiance.

1. Parks & Outdoor Adventures: Zurich features a fantastic selection of parks that tempt families to immerse themselves in nature. The Zurich Zoo serves as a perfect example, where youngsters may experience exotic species and learn about world biodiversity. Lindenhof Hill, a historic Roman fortress site, provides panoramic views of the city and a calm setting for a family picnic. The beautiful expanse of Uetliberg Mountain welcomes families to climb, ride, or just take a leisurely walk in the Swiss environment.

2. Museums for All Ages: Cultural discovery is made entertaining for the whole family in Zurich. The Swiss National Museum celebrates the Swiss past via captivating exhibits and interactive displays. The Museum of Digital Art (MuDA) provides a contemporary twist, presenting visitors with the digital world's aesthetic qualities. For those interested in technology, the Swiss Museum of Transport provides a diversity of vehicles and exhibitions that are both instructive and amusing.

3. Interactive Learning and Creativity: Families seeking engaging activities will find lots of possibilities in Zurich. The Technorama Science Center delivers hands-on activities and scientific presentations that stimulate young minds. Jugendkultur Haus Dynamo is a creative center that provides seminars, performances, and events catering to many interests, enabling children and teens to discover their artistic skills.

4. Lake Zurich: The tranquil Lake Zurich is a center of leisure activity. Families may enjoy boat excursions, picnics on the coast, or perhaps a leisurely swim during the warmer months. The nearby promenades are great for strolls, with playgrounds and open places for youngsters to play freely.

5. Gastronomic Delights for All Tastes: Zurich's gastronomic scene is not to be underestimated, and it fits even the youngest palates. Confiserie Sprüngli, a famous chocolatier, provides delightful delights that youngsters and adults alike may relish. The city's numerous eateries serve foreign cuisine, ensuring that every family member finds something to love.

6. Festivals & Events: Throughout the year, Zurich offers a range of family-friendly festivals and events. The Zurich Film Festival comprises screenings and activities for all ages, while the Zurich Street Food Festival tantalizes taste buds with foreign delicacies. The Sechseläuten spring celebration comprises a colorful procession, horsemanship shows, and the customary burning of the "Böögg" to welcome the warmer months.

7. Public Transportation Convenience: Zurich's excellent public transportation system guarantees that families may simply explore the city. The trams, buses, and trains are not only timely and pleasant but also geared to accommodate strollers and young passengers.

In essence, Zurich overcomes its status as a financial powerhouse and exposes its friendly embrace for families. Whether it's the interactive museums, huge parks, or culinary pleasures, the city offers a warm welcome for families to explore, learn, and make memorable experiences. With its ideal combination of metropolitan elegance and family-friendly charm, Zurich stands as a tribute to the notion that a cosmopolitan city can be a sanctuary for all generations.

Kid-centric attractions: Zurich Zoo, Swiss National Museum, etc.

Zurich, a city famed for its financial prowess and cultural past, offers a hidden treasure trove of kid-centric activities that appeal to the youngest adventurers. Amidst its cobblestone lanes and old buildings,

Zurich's offers reach well beyond the conventional, welcoming the curiosity and wonder of youngsters. From the magical world of the Zurich Zoo to the riveting displays of the Swiss National Museum, and beyond, families are treated to a great selection of activities that engage, educate, and amuse young minds.

1. Zurich Zoo:
Where Nature Comes Alive:

At the heart of Zurich's kid-centric attractions is the Zurich Zoo, a refuge of biodiversity and enchantment. Spanning over 17 hectares, this amazing zoo immerses youngsters in a world of animal variety, creating a profound respect for the natural world. What sets this zoo distinct is its focus on establishing genuine habitats that replicate animals' original settings. From the Kaeng Krachan Elephant Park, where beautiful elephants walk freely, to the Masoala Rainforest Hall, where youngsters may experience a piece of Madagascar's lush ecosystem, every step is a voyage of discovery.

Interactive interactions are a hallmark of the Zurich Zoo. Children may join in feeding sessions, connect with zookeepers, and even touch animals like goats and bunnies at the Kinderzoo. The Masoala Rainforest Hall invites young explorers to explore a tropical habitat, replete with waterfalls and unusual species. Conservation lessons are delicately woven throughout the experience, teaching youngsters about the significance of safeguarding animals and their habitats.

2. Swiss National Museum:
A Time Travel Through Swiss Heritage:

For families wanting a taste of history and culture, the Swiss National Museum is a riveting location. Housed in a fairy-tale castle-like edifice, this museum carries visitors, especially the youngest ones, through Switzerland's rich history. Interactive exhibitions engage youngsters in the stories of knights, castles, and folk customs, bringing Swiss history to life.

The museum's aim to make history accessible is apparent in its themed rooms. The Castle Realm gives a peek at medieval life, replete with knight's armor, while the Treasure Chamber shows the nation's most priceless relics. Children may put on costumes, touch reproductions, and engage in activities that establish a connection to the past.

3. Technorama:

Igniting Curiosity via Science: The Technorama Science Center is a sanctuary for youthful minds eager for inquiry and experimentation. Located just outside Zurich, this interactive scientific museum takes learning to new heights. Through hands-on activities and immersive displays, children may dig into the mysteries of physics, biology, and technology.

Technorama's exhibitions enable youngsters to play, question, and learn via experience. The Globus exhibit, for instance, enables students to study the Earth's rotation using huge spinning globes, while the Electricity and Magnetism section helps children comprehend the foundations of these natural forces. The museum's idea of learning by doing creates a feeling of wonder and stimulates critical thinking in children of all ages.

4. Zurich Toy Museum: Nostalgic Delights for All Ages:

The Zurich Toy Museum taps into the ageless pleasure of play and imagination. Nestled in a historic structure, this museum shows a wonderful collection of toys from various decades, delivering a nostalgic trip through childhood. From antique dolls and teddy bears to model trains and old board games, every nook is a reminder of the universality of play.

The museum's charm resides in its capacity to engage both youngsters and adults. Young visitors may marvel at the complexities of classic toys, while older generations can enjoy a walk down memory lane. The interactive areas, where youngsters may connect with traditional toys, further underscore the significance of creativity and hands-on play.

5. Kinder Museum:
Where Kids Shape Their World:

The Kinder Museum, situated inside the Swiss National Museum, is an homage to children's ingenuity and curiosity. This room encourages young visitors to develop their creative skills and interact with history via hands-on activities. Whether it's dressing up in historical costumes, producing medieval crafts, or constructing complicated constructions, the Kinder Museum invites youngsters to alter their environment through creativity and expression.

By integrating learning with play, the Kinder Museum creates a feeling of ownership over history and culture. Children are encouraged to research, create, and learn in a setting that honors their unique viewpoints.

Family-friendly restaurants and activities

Zurich, the charming jewel tucked in the heart of Switzerland, is recognized for its rich history, gorgeous scenery, and financial strength. Beyond these elements, the city provides a wealth of family-friendly food choices and activities that appeal to tourists of all ages. From scrumptious culinary experiences that thrill young palates to engaging activities that build treasured memories, Zurich's family-friendly offers are a testimony to its dedication to being a welcome destination for families.

Family-Friendly Dining: A Culinary Adventure for All Ages

Zurich's culinary industry stretches well beyond its financial sector, catering to the different interests and preferences of families. The city's restaurants, cafés, and food markets provide a potpourri of alternatives that guarantee even the youngest customers are thrilled.

Swiss Delights for Kids: Traditional Swiss food is not only delectable but also family-friendly. Dishes like Rösti, a crunchy potato dish, and Fondue, a shared melted cheese treat, provide both novelty and comfort. Many restaurants provide children's menus, providing smaller amounts of Swiss classics with popular foreign selections.

Global Flavors, Local Charm: Zurich's diverse culture is reflected in its eating selections. Families may enjoy several ethnic meals, from Italian spaghetti and

Japanese sushi to Mexican tacos and Middle Eastern kebabs. This variety assures that every family member may find something to excite their taste senses.

Cafes & Bakeries: Zurich's cafes and bakeries provide pleasant havens for families to indulge in sweet delights and soothing drinks. Confiserie Sprüngli tempts with exquisite chocolates and pastries, while local bakeries give freshly baked products that make for excellent on-the-go snacks for family outings.

Engaging Family Activities: Building Memories Together

Beyond its culinary expertise, Zurich is packed with family-oriented activities that merge entertainment and education, ensuring that children and parents alike enjoy a memorable time.

Zurich Zoo: The Zurich Zoo serves as a symbol of family-friendly entertainment. Children may view exotic creatures from throughout the globe in well-kept environments. Interactive displays, such as the Kinderzoo, where youngsters may engage with gentle animals, give a hands-on learning experience.

Parks & Outdoor Adventures: Zurich's parks provide a breath of fresh air and infinite chances for outdoor pleasure. Families may visit Uetliberg Mountain for climbing and spectacular panoramic views, or explore the vast Lindenhof Hill, a historic Roman fortress site transformed into a refuge for picnics and play.

Lake Zurich Activities: Lake Zurich is a center of family-friendly activities. Boat excursions, lakeside lunches, and strolls along the promenades offer a calm backdrop for valuable family time. During summer, the lake allows for swimming and relaxing by the water.

Museums Tailored for Children: Zurich's museums appeal to young minds hungry for inquiry. The Technorama Science Center enables children to participate in hands-on experiments, while the Kinder Museum at the Swiss National Museum empowers them to discover history via creative activities.

Festivals & Events: Zurich's family-friendly calendar is filled with festivals and events that provide something for everyone. The Zurich Film Festival features screenings and activities for youngsters, while the Zurich Street Food Festival tempts with a range of worldwide delicacies.

Navigating Zurich's Family-Friendly Delights: Public Transportation and Accessibility

Zurich's excellent public transit infrastructure ensures that families can explore the city with ease. Trams, buses, and trains are family-friendly, accommodating strollers and young visitors, making it easier to reach numerous sights and eating locations.

Chapter 13:

Local Events and Festivals

Zurich, a city steeped in history, culture, and cosmopolitan appeal, comes alive via its colorful tapestry of local events and festivals. Beyond its famed financial center and stunning scenery, Zurich features a year-round program of celebrations that highlight art, music, gastronomy, and customs. From the colorful revelry of the Zurich Street Parade to the creative display of the Zurich Film Festival, the city's local events and festivals provide insight into its vibrant character and deep-rooted legacy.

1. Zurich Street Parade: A Burst of Color and Music:

The Zurich Street Parade, one of Europe's most renowned electronic music events, turns the city into a kaleidoscope of colors and rhythms. Held annually in August, this open-air spectacular draws thousands of electronic music aficionados from across the globe. Party floats, decked with vivid decorations, traverse the streets while DJs broadcast catchy melodies, creating an exciting atmosphere.

The Street Parade is more than simply a music festival; it's a celebration of togetherness, variety, and independence. Participants dress in innovative costumes, dance in the streets, and enjoy the spirit of cooperation. The event's theme of love, tolerance, and respect connects with guests of all ages, making it a family-friendly gathering that represents Zurich's modern worldview.

2. Zurich Film Festival: A Cinematic Journey:

Every fall, the Zurich Film Festival turns the city into a powerhouse of cinematic creation.

recognized in 2005, this prominent event honors both recognized and new artists in the film business. The festival displays a broad range of films, ranging from international blockbusters to indie treasures, appealing to cinema fans of all ages.

What sets the Zurich Film Festival distinctive is its dedication to engaging spectators beyond the screen. Alongside film screenings, the festival features workshops, panel discussions, and Q&A sessions with directors and actors. The ZFF for Kids program educates younger audiences about the wonder of the film via child-friendly screenings and interactive activities.

3. Sechseläuten: Welcoming Spring with Tradition: Sechseläuten, Zurich's traditional spring celebration, harks back to medieval times. Held on the third Monday of April, the celebration centered upon the burning of the "Böögg," a snowman effigy. As the effigy burns, villagers and tourists relish in the sight, anticipating the exact time when the Böögg's head bursts, forecasting the weather for the next summer.

Sechseläuten balances heritage with contemporary. The celebration comprises a vibrant procession with guilds in medieval clothing, horsemanship shows, and beautiful floats. Families may enjoy the colorful environment, eat local food, and engage in activities that pay respect to Zurich's cultural history.

4. Zurich Christmas Market: Embracing the Festive Spirit: As winter settles upon Zurich, the city turns into a winter wonderland with the Zurich Christmas Market. The market, situated against the background of old buildings, oozes warmth and magic. Visitors may walk through wooden chalets decked with dazzling lights, uncovering artisan souvenirs, seasonal delicacies, and mulled wine.

Children are at the core of the Christmas Market's attractiveness. The Fairy Tale Tram provides young passengers with a wonderful trip through lighted streets, while the Märlitram contains storytellers who deliver fantastic stories. The market's ice rink invites families to glide beneath the open sky, making precious moments in the festive environment.

5. Food Festivals: A Gastronomic Delight:

Zurich's culinary skill takes center stage at its food festivals. The Zurich Food Festival promotes the city's gastronomic variety, bringing together local chefs, foreign cuisines, and artisanal goods. Families may go on a culinary trip, experiencing world delicacies and discovering new sensations.

6. Theater Spektakel: Celebrating Performing Arts:

The Zurich Theater Spektakel is a mixed performing arts event that highlights the city's creative energy. Held in August and September, the festival features a variety of events, from theater and dance to music and visual arts. Families may witness engaging concerts in open-air locations, enabling youngsters to participate in the arts in a unique environment.

7. Kinderumzug: A Children's Parade of Joy:

The Kinderumzug is a joyous event that provides youngsters the chance to be part of a procession during the Zurich Street procession. Children wear bright costumes, dance to music, and enjoy a joyous parade that honors their unlimited energy and inventiveness.

In essence, Zurich's local events and festivals form a vivid tapestry that symbolizes the city's liveliness and cultural diversity. These festivals enable residents and tourists alike to enjoy the spirit of togetherness, creativity, and tradition. From electronic rhythms to cinematic masterpieces, from ancient rites to gourmet pleasures, Zurich's events and festivals provide a compelling tour through its heart and soul.

Calendar of yearly events, festivals, and celebrations

Zurich, a bustling city set in the heart of Switzerland, is a cultural powerhouse that features a rich schedule of yearly events, festivals, and festivities. With a great combination of history and contemporary, Zurich provides something for everyone, from art aficionados to music fans and gourmet specialists. Let's take a tour around the year, discovering the various tapestry of festivals that decorate the city.

January - New Year's Celebrations: The year gets out with a boom as Zurich joins the globe in celebrating New Year's Eve. The legendary fireworks over Lake Zurich brighten the night sky, reflecting on the water's surface, producing a spectacular display. Locals and visitors congregate to celebrate the new year with festivals, parties, and a bustling atmosphere that engulfs the city.

February - Zurich Film Festival: February delivers cinematic enjoyment with the Zurich Film Festival. This festival gathers directors, actors, and film aficionados from across the world. The festival features a varied collection of films, from major blockbusters to avant-garde productions. It gives a forum for young talents to display their work and offers a unique chance to participate in talks and seminars with industry leaders.

March - Sechseläuten: As winter bids adieu and spring fills the city with vivid colors, Zurich celebrates Sechseläuten. This traditional spring event focuses on the

Böögg, a snowman-like figure loaded with explosives. As the figure is set to fire, people excitedly anticipate the moment when the head bursts, signaling the approach of warmer months. The celebration is a vibrant combination of historical reenactments, parades, and gastronomic pleasures.

April - Street Food Festival: Zurich's culinary talent takes the limelight in April with the Street Food Festival. This festival brings together a multitude of food trucks and kiosks serving an assortment of ethnic cuisines. From gourmet burgers to exotic Asian cuisine and scrumptious desserts, travelers may go on a culinary adventure that represents the city's varied nature.

May - Zurich Marathon: Fitness enthusiasts and professional runners alike come in May for the Zurich Marathon. The event features different racing categories, including the full marathon, half marathon, and relay events.

Participants explore the city's picturesque pathways, passing prominent attractions such as Lake Zurich and the Old Town. The marathon develops a feeling of community and healthy rivalry among residents and guests.

June - Zurich Festival: The Zurich Festival, held in June, is a celebration of the arts in all its manifestations. This month-long event comprises theater plays, music concerts, dance acts, and visual arts exhibits. Renowned artists and new talents unite to offer a dynamic cultural experience that embodies Zurich's creative energy.

July - Street Parade: Electrifying music, bright costumes, and a throbbing atmosphere characterize the Street Parade, one of Europe's major techno music events. In July, the streets of Zurich change into a dance floor as electronic music aficionados from across the globe unite to celebrate

195

togetherness, variety, and freedom of expression.

August - Zurich Pride Festival: Diversity and inclusiveness take center stage in August during the Zurich Pride Festival. This festival supports LGBTQ+ rights and visibility via marches, dialogues, art displays, and performances. It's a moment for celebration, contemplation, and activism as Zurich confirms its commitment to equal rights and respect.

September - Knabenschiessen: A distinctive Zurich tradition, the Knabenschiessen, is a shooting tournament going back to the Middle Ages. Held in September, this tournament brings together marksmen of all ages to display their shooting talents. While the initial event centered on young boys, it has developed into an inclusive tournament for all locals, encouraging friendship and friendly rivalry.

October - Zurich Game Show: Gaming fans and technology connoisseurs congregate for the Zurich Game Show in October. This event celebrates the world of gaming, showcasing the newest video games, virtual reality experiences, e-sports tournaments, and interactive exhibitions. It's a paradise for gamers and a tribute to Zurich's embracing of innovation.

November - Zurich Illuminarium: As the days become shorter and winter approaches, Zurich holds the Luminarium in November. The city is covered with spectacular light works, converting its streets and monuments into a wonderful fantasy. The Illumination encompasses the festive mood, preparing the city for the forthcoming holiday season.

December - Christmas Markets: The year comes full circle with the charming Christmas markets that grace Zurich's streets in December. These markets create a festive ambiance, with merchants offering homemade crafts, mulled wine, and holiday delicacies. The perfume of cinnamon and spices permeates the air as tourists immerse themselves in the pleasant environment of the festive season.

Insider advice for experiencing local customs

Zurich, a city that brilliantly mixes history and contemporary, is a treasure mine of local customs waiting to be found. As you tour this dynamic Swiss city, immersing yourself in its cultural legacy will improve your experience. Here are some insider recommendations to help you completely embrace and appreciate the local customs of Zurich.

1. Embrace the Culinary Delights: Swiss cuisine is more than simply chocolate and cheese, and Zurich offers a delightful assortment of classic delicacies. Start your day with a full Swiss breakfast, comprising muesli, fresh bread, and local cheeses. Don't miss the chance to sample fondue, a communal eating experience when you dip bread into a pot of melted cheese. To completely immerse oneself, visit traditional Swiss eateries and pubs, known as "Zunfthäuser," which give a taste of true local cuisine.

2. Experience the Sechseläuten Parade:

The Sechseläuten Parade, held in March, is a treasured Zurich institution that heralds the entrance of spring. To properly appreciate this spectacle, come early to acquire a good viewing place along the parade route. Immerse yourself in the joyful atmosphere as ancient guilds, musicians, and entertainers demonstrate their abilities. The climax is the burning of the Böögg, which represents the end of winter and the prospect of warmer days.

3. Visit the Farmer's Markets: To engage with Zurich's local culinary culture, tour its busy farmer's markets. The biggest, Wochenmarkt Bellevue, provides a range of fresh vegetables, artisanal items, and regional delicacies. Engage with sellers and locals, and embrace the chance to try and buy real Swiss ingredients to take home as mementos.

4. Attend the Street Parade: For a memorable experience in August, attend the Street Parade, one of Europe's biggest techno music events. Dive into the vivid environment, dress in colorful apparel, and dance to the electronic sounds. Engage with the varied audience, and celebrate togetherness, variety, and freedom of speech. To truly enjoy the event, remain hydrated, and acquaint yourself with the parade route and transportation alternatives.

5. Participate in the Knabenschiessen: To obtain a view of Zurich's historical origins, try visiting the Knabenschiessen, a classic shooting tournament held in September. This event, going back to the Middle Ages, is accessible to marksmen of all ages. While appreciating the competitive spirit, immerse yourself in the camaraderie and customs that have been handed down through centuries.

6. Discover Swiss Chocolate Secrets: While Swiss chocolate is recognized globally, Zurich provides unique methods to savor this favorite dessert. Take a chocolate-making session to learn about the art of manufacturing chocolate from scratch. Additionally, tour the city's chocolate shops, some of which have been creating these delightful delicacies for decades. Engage with chocolatiers, try various types, and receive insights into the delicate chocolate-making process.

7. Explore Christmas Markets: In December, Zurich's Christmas markets produce a magnificent ambiance that encapsulates the spirit of the festive season. To thoroughly experience this tradition, tour various markets situated around the city. Engage with craftsmen, browse for handcrafted products, and sample seasonal delights like roasted chestnuts and mulled wine. Take in the beautiful light displays and immerse yourself in the festive mood.

8. Embrace Cultural events: Throughout the year, Zurich offers a range of cultural events that give a chance to connect with local customs. Attend the Zurich Festival for a varied choice of artistic acts, or join the Zurich Pride Festival to celebrate diversity and inclusiveness. Engage with locals and other tourists, and receive insights into Zurich's diverse cultural scene.

9. Use Public Transportation: To truly enjoy Zurich's unique customs, travel the city utilizing its efficient public transportation system. This will enable you to explore the city like a native, connect with locals, and observe the everyday rhythm of Zurich life. Additionally, public transit will take you to many traditional and cultural sites without the inconvenience of parking.

10. Engage with Locals: The most genuine approach to experiencing local customs is through engaging with Zurich's locals. Strike up talks with locals in cafés, markets, and events. Ask for suggestions, learn about their practices, and embrace the chance to develop significant contacts that will expand your awareness of Zurich's cultural tapestry.

Chapter 14.

Practical Information

Zurich, the biggest city in Switzerland, is a bustling metropolis that perfectly integrates its rich past with contemporary urban life. With its gorgeous scenery, cultural attractions, and efficient public services, Zurich provides an exceptional experience for both visitors and inhabitants alike. This book gives practical information to help you navigate and make the most of your stay in this interesting city.

1. Getting There and Around
Zurich is well-connected to the globe via Zurich Airport, one of the busiest airports in Europe. From the airport, you may easily reach the city center by train, tram, and bus. The city's public transit system is famous for its efficiency and regularity. The Zurich Card

enables unlimited travel on public transit, including trains, trams, and buses, as well as free or subsidized entrance to numerous museums and attractions.

2. Accommodation

Zurich provides a variety of housing alternatives, from luxury hotels to budget-friendly hostels. The center sections, such as the Old Town and the Bahnhofstrasse retail district, are popular locations to stay in owing to their closeness to key attractions. It's advisable to reserve your accommodation in advance, particularly during busy tourist seasons.

3. Currency and Payment

The currency used in Zurich and across Switzerland is the Swiss Franc (CHF). Credit and debit cards are frequently accepted, however, it's advised to bring extra cash for smaller businesses and markets. ATMs are easily accessible around the city.

4. Language

The official languages of Zurich are Swiss German, French, Italian, and Romansh. English is also frequently spoken, especially in tourist regions, making communication reasonably simple for travelers.

5. Attractions and Activities

Zurich provides a wealth of attractions to satisfy all interests. The Old Town (Altstadt) is a must-visit, with its medieval architecture, tiny lanes, and historical attractions. The famed Lake Zurich gives chances for boat rides, lakeside strolls, and picnics with a view of the Alps. For art connoisseurs, the Kunsthaus Zurich offers an excellent collection of Swiss and worldwide art.

6. Culinary Delights

Zurich's culinary culture reflects its multinational nature. While Swiss cuisine is a combination of distinct regional delicacies, you'll also discover worldwide tastes in the shape of restaurants, cafés, and street food carts. Don't miss sampling fondue, a typical Swiss meal of melted cheese served with bread pieces for dipping.

7. Shopping

Zurich is a shopper's paradise, with the famed Bahnhofstrasse being one of the world's most upscale retail avenues. Here, you'll discover luxury shops, worldwide brands, and department stores. For unusual gifts, visit the Old Town's boutique stores and marketplaces.

8. Healthcare

Zurich provides high-quality healthcare services. European travelers may utilize the European Health Insurance Card (EHIC) for emergency medical care. Non-European travelers should have adequate travel insurance that covers medical expenditures.

9. Safety

Zurich is regarded as one of the safest cities in the world. However, as in any other city, it's essential to keep alert of your surroundings and take normal safety precautions, such as securing your valuables and avoiding poorly lighted areas at night.

10. Climate

Zurich enjoys a moderate climate with distinct seasons. Summers (June to August) are delightfully mild, but winters (December to February) are chilly and snowy. It's vital to dress in layers and be prepared for rapid weather changes, especially in the shoulder seasons.

Accommodation alternatives for varied budgets

Zurich, the lovely Swiss city perched at the foot of the Alps, welcomes tourists from all walks of life. Whether you're a backpacker on a shoestring budget or a luxury seeker, Zurich provides a broad choice of lodging alternatives to appeal to any traveler's demands. From lovely hostels to magnificent hotels, this guide can help you navigate the city's lodging scene depending on your budget.

Budget-Friendly Options:

Hostels: For budget-conscious tourists, hostels are a good alternative. Zurich features numerous well-maintained hostels that provide economical dormitory-style accommodations or individual rooms for a fraction of the cost of hotels. Hostels like

"Zurich Youth Hostel" and **"Langstars Backpackers"** give pleasant lodgings, public facilities, and an opportunity to meet other visitors.

Guesthouses & Budget Hotels: You'll discover a choice of guesthouses and budget hotels that give warm and cheap accommodations. These facilities generally provide basic amenities and a pleasant stay without breaking the wallet. Consider venues like **"Hotel Marta"** and **"Hotel Limmathof"** for a wallet-friendly stay in the center of the city.

Mid-Range Options:

Boutique Hotels: Zurich is home to various boutique hotels that provide a blend of flair and comfort without the high price tag. These hotels frequently include distinctive design, individualized service, and well-appointed rooms. Check out choices like **"Hotel Seehof**" and **"Hotel Adler**" for a mid-range boutique experience.

Apartment Rentals: Another option to explore is renting an apartment or serviced flat. This is a wonderful alternative for those wanting additional room, solitude, and the convenience of a kitchen. Websites like Airbnb and Booking.com provide a choice of housing possibilities in Zurich.

Luxury Options:

Luxury Hotels: Zurich provides a range of world-class luxury hotels that offer flawless service, opulent suites, and magnificent views. If your money permits, luxuriate in the magnificence of hotels like the legendary **"Baur au Lac"**, the exquisite **"The Dolder Grand"**, or the smart **"Park Hyatt Zurich"**.

Spa Resorts: For a sumptuous experience, try staying at one of Zurich's spa resorts.

These magnificent getaways provide top-notch amenities, wellness facilities, and a tranquil ambiance. The **"Widder Hotel"** and the "Atlantis by Giardino" are famous for their spa and wellness offers.

Tips for Booking Accommodation:

Book in Advance: Zurich is a popular tourist destination, particularly during high seasons. To ensure your favorite hotel at the best prices, it's important to book well in advance.

Flexible Dates: If your trip dates are flexible, try coming during the shoulder seasons (spring and autumn) when hotel rates tend to be cheaper, and the city is less busy.

Location: While hotels in the city center provide convenience, try staying in somewhat less central places to obtain cheaper bargains without compromising accessibility thanks to Zurich's effective public transit system.

Package packages: Some hotels offer package packages that include lodgings, food, and access to attractions. These may give excellent value for money.

Essential contact information: hospitals, embassies, emergency services

When going to a new place, it's necessary to have access to critical contact information for emergencies, medical aid, and diplomatic support. Zurich, the cultural and financial heart of Switzerland, is a friendly place that values the safety and well-being of its citizens and tourists. This guide contains crucial contact information for hospitals, embassies, and emergency services in Zurich, ensuring that you're well-prepared for any circumstance throughout your visit.

1. Hospitals and Medical Assistance:

University Hospital Zurich (USZ):
Address: Rämistrasse 100, 8091 Zurich
Emergency Contact: 24/7 Emergency
Department **Phone:** +41 44 255 11 11

Triemli Hospital:
Address: Birmensdorferstrasse 497, 8063
Zurich **Emergency Contact:** 24/7
Emergency Department **Phone:** +41 44 466
11 11

Hirslanden Klinik Im Park:
Address: Seestrasse 220, 8027
Zurich Phone: +41 44 209 21 11

**Emergency Medical Services
(Rettungsdienst):** For urgent medical help,
call 144 from any phone. This service links
you to emergency medical services, offering
quick support in medical crises.

2. Embassies and Consulates:

United States Embassy:
Address: Sulgeneckstrasse 19, 3007
Bern Phone: +41 31 357 70 11

British Embassy:
Address: Thunstrasse 50, 3005
Bern Phone: +41 31 359 77 00

Embassy of Canada: Address:
Kirchenfeldstrasse 88, 3005
Bern Phone: +41 31 357 32 00

Embassy of Australia:
Address: Kirchenfeldstrasse 73, 3005
Bern Phone: +41 31 350 15 45

Emergency Services:
Police: For quick police help, call 117 from any phone.

Fire Department: In case of a fire emergency, call 118 from any phone.

Emergency Medical Services: For medical emergencies, call 144 from any phone.

Emergency Response for Accident and Poisoning: In case of accidents or poisoning, ring 145 from any phone.

Roadside help: For roadside help or car breakdowns, call 140 from any phone.

Important Tips:

Language: The official languages of Zurich are Swiss German, French, Italian, and Romansh. In emergency circumstances, operators answering emergency lines are likely to understand English, but it's important to know crucial words in the local language as well.

identity: Keep a copy of your identity, travel papers, and any medical information ready.

These might be useful during emergencies and hospital visits.

Travel Insurance: Before flying to Zurich, make sure you have comprehensive travel insurance that covers medical bills, repatriation, and other emergency services.

Local Contacts: Save the emergency numbers in your phone contacts and have a paper copy in your wallet or handbag for rapid access.

Consular Services: Embassies and consulates may give help in case of lost passports, legal concerns, and other crises affecting your home country's inhabitants.

Chapter 15.

Language and Etiquette

Zurich, a city set inside the stunning terrain of Switzerland, is not only famed for its magnificent beauty and financial prowess but also for its unique language and etiquette. The cultural fabric of Zurich is woven with a rich past that impacts its language variety and the exquisite manners that characterize its social interactions. This note tries to go into the complexities of Zurich's linguistic variants and the various etiquettes that form interpersonal connections within this dynamic metropolis.

Language variety: Zurich's linguistic variety is reminiscent of Switzerland's multilingual background. While the official languages of Switzerland are German, French, Italian, and Romansh, the predominant language spoken in Zurich is Swiss German. However, it's vital to realize that Swiss German differs greatly from standard German, both in pronunciation and vocabulary. This dialect is firmly engrained in Zurich's culture since it exhibits a distinct personality that differentiates it from other German-speaking places.

Despite the prominence of Swiss German, many Zurich inhabitants are skilled in English owing to the city's cosmopolitan character and its position as a worldwide financial center. English is commonly utilized in commercial and professional environments, making it a vital tool for communication.

Etiquette & Social Norms: Zurich's etiquette is defined by a combination of traditional traditions and contemporary sensibilities. Punctuality is highly respected, and being on time for appointments or social occasions is vital. This timeliness demonstrates regard for others' time and responsibilities, and it's considered disrespectful to keep someone waiting.

When engaged in discussion, keeping a certain amount of formality is necessary. Addressing persons using their titles and surnames, followed by a courteous "Mr." or "Ms.," is traditional until a more comfortable rapport is developed. A solid handshake and direct eye contact are regarded as signals of sincerity and respect during greetings.

Dining etiquette in Zurich follows European norms. Table manners are maintained methodically, with the right use of utensils and the avoidance of speaking with food in one's mouth. Tipping is common, however, it's often included in the bill. It's also crucial to participate in meaningful discussions during meals since exchanging opinions and ideas develops a feeling of togetherness.

Cultural Sensitivity: Respecting Zurich's cultural variety is crucial. The Swiss are noted for their reserved disposition, respecting personal space and solitude. Approaching individuals in a calm and cool manner is welcomed, and avoiding highly expressive movements is encouraged, since they may be seen as intrusive.

Furthermore, clothing requirements are generally adhered to, especially in professional and formal contexts. Wearing a modest dress is essential to demonstrate respect for local traditions and preserve a professional image.

Gender Equality: Zurich's modern culture lays a high focus on gender equality. Women have prominent roles in several industries, including business and government. It's vital to address people based on their professional titles and accomplishments rather than their gender, reflecting the city's dedication to breaking down gender barriers.

Basic Swiss German phrases and linguistic hints

Zurich, tucked in the heart of Switzerland, captivates travelers with its breathtaking scenery and dynamic culture. While English is frequently spoken, having a grasp of basic Swiss German phrases may enrich your experience and connect you with locals on a deeper level. This note is your entry to acquiring important Swiss-German phrases and navigating the linguistic terrain of Zurich with confidence.

1. Greetings and Basic Phrases: Mastering greetings is the first step to engaging with the people of Zurich. Here are some basic Swiss German phrases:

Hello! (Hello!)
Guten Tag! (Good day!)

Wie geht's? (How are you?) Danke! (Thank you) Bitte! (Please/You're welcome) Entschuldigung! (Excuse me/I'm sorry) Ja (Yes) / Nei (No)

Wie heisst du? (What's your name?)

Ich heisse... (My name is...)

Sprechen Sie Englisch? (Do you speak English?)

2. Numbers and Directions:

Navigating Zurich is simpler with basic numbers and guiding words at your fingertips:

Eins, Zwei, Drei (One, Two, Three)

Links (Left) / Rechts (Right)

Geradeaus (Straight forward)

Wo ist...? (Where is...?)

Ich suche... (I'm seeking for...)

Bahnstation (Train station)

Flughafen (Airport)

Toilette (Restroom)

3. Ordering Food and Shopping:

Exploring Zurich's food scene and shopping becomes more pleasurable with these phrases:

Die Speisekarte, bitte. (The menu, please.) Ich möchte... (I would like...) Essen (Food) / Trinken (Drink) Eine Tasse Kaffee (A cup of coffee) Wie viel kostet das? (How much does it cost?) Kann ich mit Kreditkarte bezahlen? (Can I pay with a credit card?) Einkaufszentrum (Shopping Center) Wie spät ist es? (What time is it?)

4. Language Tips for Zurich: Navigating the subtleties of Swiss German may be both fun and rewarding. Here are some linguistic guidelines to bear in mind:

Dialect Variation: Swiss German may differ from area to region. While Zurich's Swiss German provides an excellent basis, don't be shocked if you meet subtle variances while visiting other areas of Switzerland.

Politeness: Swiss society lays considerable significance on politeness and etiquette. Use titles and last names, and opt for "Sie" (formal 'you') until requested to use "du" (informal 'you').

Pronunciation: Swiss German pronunciation may vary from standard German. Consonants could be quieter, and vowel sounds can shift. Practice with locals or listen to native speakers for correct pronunciation.

Context Matters: Swiss German phrases may have distinct meanings in diverse settings. Pay attention to the circumstance and tone to ensure you're utilizing the proper term.

Practice with Locals: Engage with locals in easy dialogues. Most would appreciate your attempt to speak their language, even if you're not proficient.

Cultural etiquette and dos and don'ts for guests

Zurich, with its combination of historic beauty and contemporary refinement, invites tourists from throughout the globe. However, to completely immerse oneself in this dynamic Swiss city, learning its cultural etiquette is important. Navigating social conventions, habits, and traditions guarantees a courteous and enjoyable encounter. This letter acts as your cultural compass, leading you through the dos and don'ts of Zurich's social scene.

1. Punctuality and Respect for Time: In Zurich, punctuality is more than a virtue; it's a way of life. Arriving on time for appointments, meetings, and social engagements is a demonstration of respect for others' time and obligations. Be careful to arrange your activities properly and alert hosts if you're running late.

2. Greeting Etiquette: Zurich's greeting etiquette reflects its combination of formality and tenderness. A vigorous handshake and close eye contact are usual during greetings. Address persons using their titles and surnames followed by a courteous "Mr." or "Ms." until a more comfortable rapport is developed. A courteous inclination of the head is also an acceptable greeting.

3. Social Boundaries and Personal Space: Respect for personal space is a cornerstone of Zurich's etiquette. The Swiss are noted for their reserved temperament, favoring a comfortable physical distance during encounters. While talks are encouraged, avoid unnecessary motions and keep a controlled posture.

4. Dining Etiquette: Dining in Zurich is a cultural event that involves respect for particular etiquette norms:

Table Manners: Practice excellent table manners, including using utensils properly and abstaining from chatting with food in your mouth.

Tipping: Tipping is traditional, albeit not mandatory, since a service fee may be included in the bill. Leaving a little tip is appreciated for outstanding service.

Dress Code: Dress modestly and properly, particularly at luxury restaurants or formal settings. Wearing modest clothes indicates respect for local norms.

Conversations: Engage in meaningful conversation throughout meals, demonstrating genuine interest in people and their viewpoints. Meals are generally a time for social contact and engagement.

5. Language Considerations: While English is commonly spoken in Zurich, making an effort to learn a few basic Swiss

German phrases will gain you respect and admiration from locals. Learning to say "hello," "thank you," and simple words may go a long way in developing connections.

6. Gender Equality and Respect: Zurich has a proactive position on gender equality. When talking with people, concentrate on their professional credentials and accomplishments rather than their gender. This strategy resonates with Zurich's inclusive principles.

Dos:

Do Embrace Punctuality: Being on time indicates respect for others' schedules.

Do Practice Good Table Manners: Adhere to eating decorum and participate in meaningful discussions.

Do Use Basic Swiss German Phrases: Efforts to speak the local language are welcomed.

Do Respect Personal Space: Maintain a reasonable space throughout interactions.

Do Address People Formally: Use titles and surnames in formal situations until a stronger bond is developed.

Don'ts:

Don't Be Late: Avoid keeping people waiting; punctuality is highly prized.

Don't Interrupt: Allow others to finish speaking before adding to the discussion.

Don't Overdo motions: Maintain a cool attitude and avoid too expressive motions.

Don't Assume Gender Roles: Focus on professional accomplishments rather than gender.

Don't Neglect Dress Code: Dress cleanly and correctly, particularly in formal situations

Itinerary for 7 Days in Zurich

Day 1: Arrival and Old Town Exploration

Morning: Arrive in Zurich and check into your hotel.

Afternoon: Start your journey in Zurich's Old Town (Altstadt). Wander through its small alleyways, see Grossmünster and Fraumünster churches, and appreciate the ancient beauty.

Evening: Have supper at a local Swiss restaurant.

Day 2: Lake Zurich and Bahnhofstrasse Shopping

Morning: Take a walk around Lake Zurich's promenade or try a boat tour to appreciate the city's cityscape from the lake.

Afternoon: Visit Bahnhofstrasse, one of the world's most renowned retail avenues, for luxury shopping and people-watching.

Evening: Relax by the lake or select from Zurich's various eating choices.

Day 3: Day Trip to Lucerne

Morning: Take a train to Lucerne (about 1-hour travel).

Day: Explore Lucerne's picturesque old town, see the Chapel Bridge, and Lion Monument, and consider taking a cable car journey to Mount Pilatus for panoramic views.

Evening: Return to Zurich and relax.

Day 4: Kunsthaus Zurich and Parks

Morning: Visit Kunsthaus Zurich, one of Switzerland's most significant art museums.

Day: Spend your day at one of Zurich's gorgeous parks like Uetliberg or Botanical Garden.

Evening: Experience Zurich's lively food scene.

Day 5: Zurich Zoo and Swiss National Museum

Morning: Explore Zurich Zoo, famed for its naturalistic habitats.

Afternoon: Visit the Swiss National Museum to learn about the country's history and culture.

Evening: Enjoy a relaxed evening at a neighborhood café or take a leisurely walk along the Limmat River.

Day 6: Day Trip to Rhine Falls and Stein am Rhein

Morning: Take a train to Schaffhausen to experience Europe's tallest waterfall, Rhine Falls.

Afternoon: Continue to Stein am Rhein, a lovely medieval town famed for its well-preserved architecture.

Evening: Return to Zurich and have a goodbye meal.

Day 7: Museum Hopping and Departure

Morning: Visit several of Zurich's lesser-known museums like the Museum of Design or FIFA World Football Museum.

Afternoon: Depending on your departure schedule, you could have some spare time for last-minute shopping or leisure.

Departure: Check out of your hotel and go to the airport or train station for your onward trip.

Remember that this is a proposed schedule and may be altered depending on your tastes and interests. Also, consider verifying the opening hours and availability of attractions in advance, particularly if you're visiting during high seasons. Enjoy your vacation in Zurich!

Printed in Great Britain
by Amazon

36987578R00136